Offenders on probation

by

George Mair and Chris May

A Research and Statistics Directorate Report

Home Office
Research and
Statistics
Directorate

London: Home Office

Home Office Research Studies

The Home Office Research Studies are reports on research undertaken by or on behalf of the Home Office. They cover the range of subjects for which the Home Secretary has responsibility. Titles in the series are listed at the back of this report (copies are available from the address on the back cover). Other publications produced by the Research and Statistics Directorate include Research Findings, the Research Bulletin, Statistical Bulletins and Statistical Papers.

The Research and Statistics Directorate

The Directorate consists of three Units which deal with research and statistics on Crime and Criminal Justice, Offenders and Corrections, Immigration and General Matters; the Programme Development Unit; the Economics Unit; and the Operational Research Unit.

 The Research and Statistics Directorate is an integral part of the Home Office, serving the Ministers and the department itself, its services, Parliament and the public through research, development and statistics. Information and knowledge from these sources informs policy development and the management of programmes; their dissemination improves wider public understanding of matters of Home Office concern.

First published 1997

Application for reproduction should be made to the Information and Publications Group, Room 201, Home Office, 50 Queen Anne's Gate, London SW1H 9AT.

©Crown copyright 1997 ISBN 1 85893 890 2
ISSN 0072 6435

Foreword

In recent years, the probation service has been asked to supervise more, and more serious, offenders. At the same time the requirements upon it to demonstrate effectiveness have intensified.

To date the performance of the probation service has been assessed mainly through measuring reconviction rates following community sentences and through sentencer satisfaction surveys. This report looks at the way the service supervises through the eyes of the offenders. It examines what offenders themselves have to say about their problems, their attitudes to offending and their perceptions of the supervision process. The results show that the probation service is working with a group of people characterised by poor school attainment, high unemployment and a high incidence of previous convictions and drug usage. Despite this, the overall message of the study for the probation service is a good one: it is viewed positively by most of those it supervises, and appears to be working hard to achieve its aims of reducing reoffending and encouraging and assisting offenders to lead law-abiding lives.

CHRIS LEWIS

Head of Offenders and Corrections Unit
Research and Statistics Directorate

Acknowledgements

We would like to thank Harry Fletcher of the National Association of Probation Officers, Mike Hough of the Home Office, Ieaun Miles of Central Probation Council and Peter Patrick of Oxford Probation Service who were involved in the initial stages of planning and setting up the survey; Peter Sheriff of the Home Office for help with drawing the sample; staff of Social & Community Planning Research, in particular Jon Hales, Deborah Ghate and David Dundon-Smith for conducting the survey; and other colleagues in the Home Office, including Carol Hedderman, Sarah Rae, Julie Vennard and Roy Walmsley, for commenting on early drafts of this report.

Thanks are also due to the many probation service staff whose efforts made it possible to contact offenders. Finally, we must thank all the offenders who agreed to be interviewed.

GEORGE MAIR

CHRIS MAY

Contents

Summary

Background and methodology (Chapters 1 and 2)

Recently there has been increasing pressure on the probation service to demonstrate its effectiveness. Assessment has concentrated on reconviction studies and sentencer satisfaction surveys, but hitherto little has been known of the impact of probation from the point of view of those supervised. The study described here surveyed a sample of offenders on probation, examining the backgrounds, their experiences of probation, and their perceptions of its helpfulness in tackling problems and stopping further offending.

Social and Community Planning Research (SCPR) conducted the survey in the first half of 1994. At this time the 1992 National Standards were in place (revised standards were introduced in 1995). The survey was restricted to those who had been sentenced to a probation or combination order, and covered 22 of the then 55 probation areas in England and Wales.

The sample of offenders in each area was drawn at random. In total the issued sample consisted of 3,300 offenders. Nearly 40 per cent of the sample could not be contacted, mainly because they had been taken into custody, their order had terminated, or they had been transferred to another area. The effective sample, after subtracting those not contactable, was 1,986. Of these, 1,213 interviews were achieved, giving a response rate of 61 per cent. It is possible that those who failed to keep survey appointments will tend to have a less favourable attitude to the probation service than those included. The possibility of bias should be kept in mind when examining the findings.

Characteristics of the sample (Chapter 3)

Overall, 84 per cent of the sample were currently on a probation order only, 12 per cent were on a combination order, and four per cent were on a probation order and also serving a separate community service order. For just over half of the respondents it was their first time on probation.

Men were more likely to have been convicted of burglary, driving offences, and theft of/from cars than women; while women were more likely than men to have been convicted of theft/handling offences and fraud/forgery. Burglary and car theft was less common among older offenders, while drink-driving offences were more common. Two-thirds of respondents had been sentenced in a magistrates' court.

The sample was generally representative of all persons on probation in terms of sex (82% were male) and age (just over 40% of respondents were in the 16 to 24 age range). The average age of offenders is lower than that of the general population.

Ninety-three per cent of the sample was white, a proportion very similar to that of the general population. Of the rest, most defined themselves as black. Just over half of the sample was single, whereas in the general population (where the average age is higher) only 21 per cent of adults are single. However, in the 16 to 20 age group probationers were much more likely than this age group in the general population to be married or living as married.

Only one in five of the sample was employed or self-employed, compared with over 60 per cent of the general population of working age. Young people were more likely to be out of work than older respondents. Of those who were employed, 79 per cent were in manual occupations. About a third of female probationers were living alone with dependent children, a proportion twice as large as for both female prisoners and women of child-bearing age in the general population.

Almost one-fifth of the sample had spent time in a residential children's home, whereas only two per cent of the general population had been taken into care before the age of sixteen. Fourteen per cent of male probationers had been in a borstal or young offenders unit. Twelve per cent of male probationers had gained O levels (or equivalent), compared with 19 per cent of the general population.

Seventy per cent of respondents lived in rented accommodation, a much higher proportion than that for the general population. For two–thirds of respondents the main source of household income was state benefit. About 40 per cent had had problems with paying bills; those aged 16 to 20 were least likely to owe money on household bills, but most likely (52%) to be in debt to a person who was not a friend or relative. Only a quarter of probationers held a current full licence to drive a car, compared with about two-thirds of the general population; the difference between offenders and the general population was apparent in all age groups.

Almost half of the sample said that they currently had health problems or disabilities. About 30 per cent said that health problems limited the work that they could do; the similar figure for the general population was less than 20 per cent. The difference between the two groups was even more pronounced when the comparison was limited to those aged under 45.

Drug usage among probationers was far higher than in the general population. For example, cannabis had been used by 57 per cent of male probationers aged 16 to 29 in the last 12 months, compared with 25 per cent of this age group in the general population. Even greater differences were found for other less commonly used drugs. Nearly half the sample said they drank alcohol never or rarely. However, at the other end of the scale there appeared to be a minority for whom drinking was a problem; for example, 14 per cent said that they sometimes went on drinking binges.

Previous criminal history (Chapter 3)

Eighty-two per cent said they had been previously convicted. Men and older offenders were more likely to have been convicted. Burglary and theft were the most common offences for which respondents were first convicted, while the most common sentence was a fine. Probation was the second most common first sentence for older offenders, but fourth most common for those aged 16 to 20.

Nearly half of probationers admitted that they had offended and not been caught before being first convicted. The most common of such offences were theft/handling, burglary and car theft or theft from a car.

Beginning the current order (Chapter 4)

Eighty-five per cent of respondents said that they had been given a copy of their probation order to sign when they first started supervision, as required by national standards. Over 90 per cent said that their probation officer had made sure that they agreed to the order. Nearly 80 per cent said that they had been given a leaflet explaining what it meant to be on probation, while 12 per cent said they had not been given any written information. Over 90 per cent said that they had been told by their probation officer what would happen in the event of a breach of the order. Similar percentages applied to those starting community service orders.

The majority of probation officers appeared to be adhering to the National Standards concerning supervision plans. However, a substantial minority were not doing so: nearly 20 per cent of all respondents said that a supervision plan was not drawn up and a further 15 per cent could not remember or did not answer. Of those who said that a plan was drawn up 22 per cent said they were not given the plan and 18 per cent could not remember or did not answer.

The current probation order (Chapter 4)

The National Standards specify that the initial appointment should be arranged whenever possible within five working days of the making of the order. It appears that at least one in five offenders is not being seen within the guidelines. However, three-quarters of offenders had their first supervision session with a probation officer within the same week or the week following sentence.

The National Standards for Probation Orders suggested that where practicable, in the first three months of the order an offender should be seen by his/her supervising officer about once a week. This seems to have been followed for more than 80 per cent of the sample. Younger offenders were seen more often, but sessions for older offenders were longer.

Over half of male offenders and nearly three-quarters of female offenders were supervised by female probation officers. Both male and female offenders were more likely to be happy with female officers than with males. Almost one-third of respondents were being supervised by a different probation officer from the one seen on the first supervision session.

Content of supervision (Chapter 4)

The most commonly discussed subject in the *last* supervision session was employment (mentioned by 42% of respondents), whereas the topic most commonly discussed in *previous* sessions was 'why I committed the offence' (62%). Generally the topics discussed reflected characteristics of offenders such as health, employment and the use of alcohol.

Of projects or programmes the most commonly attended was an alcohol management and counselling group. Young offenders were more likely to have attended training/employment units, probation centres, motor projects and staying out of trouble courses than older age groups. Older offenders, however, were more likely to have attended an alcohol group, and those in their twenties were more likely to have attended a drugs group.

About a third of respondents said that their probation officer had given them help or advice with various money matters.

Views of and attitudes towards probation and probation officers (Chapter 4)

Offenders were asked why they thought they had been given a probation/combination order rather than another sentence. The most common response (27%) was that the court had wanted the offender to benefit from the services available while on probation. No-one mentioned that they had been given their current sentence to stop them reoffending.

The most frequently given 'good point' about being on probation (mentioned by more than half) was that it gave offenders access to someone independent to talk to about problems. A third of respondents mentioned getting practical help or advice with specific problems, and about 20 per cent mentioned being helped to keep out of trouble and avoid offending. The most commonly mentioned bad point was the time taken to attend supervision sessions (24%), with the inconvenience of travelling to attend (7%) being next most mentioned. These criticisms help to suggest that orders are achieving the objective of restricting liberty and punishing offenders. More than half the sample did not mention any bad points at all.

Nine out of ten respondents thought that their current probation order was either fairly or very useful. Women and older offenders were more likely to see their orders as very useful.

Respondents were shown a series of statements about probation and probation officers. More than a third agreed strongly that being on probation would help them to stop offending altogether, while a further 20 per cent agreed slightly. However, fewer than half agreed strongly that being on probation kept them out of trouble. More than 60 per cent agreed strongly with two general statements about probation officers being able to help people.

There were high levels of agreement with the positive statements about probation officers and high levels of disagreement with the negative statements. Only one in twenty respondents said anything negative about their probation officer. Three-quarters of the sample felt that they could always talk to their probation officer if they were worried about something, and nearly as many said that they felt they could be completely honest and frank. More than three-quarters of the sample said that there was nothing that they would be unwilling or embarrassed to talk about with their officer.

Nearly three-quarters of respondents said that being on probation had helped them understand their offending behaviour, and almost two-thirds said that they thought being on probation would help them stay out of trouble in the future.

Added conditions (Chapter 5)

Forty per cent of respondents said that they had attended a special programme or activity as part of their current probation order, though there was some confusion about whether such programmes were an added condition of their order or whether they were being attended voluntarily.

More than a quarter of respondents said they had attended a group of some kind as a condition of their order. Groups which dealt with alcohol problems were the most commonly attended, while groups looking at offending behaviour and motor projects were also often attended. Nearly 40 per cent of those attending said there were no bad points about groups.

Only four per cent said that they had had to live at a probation hostel as a condition of their order, and seven per cent of the sample had attended a probation centre.

Community service (Chapter 5)

Twelve per cent of the sample were on a combination order. In their last session of community service, 82 per cent of these had been working in a group, 10 per cent had been working alone, and five per cent had been working in a session run by an agency other than probation. Painting and decorating was the most common form of work, followed by gardening.

One-quarter of those who had done community service said that it had no good points at all, seeing it as an inconvenience and restriction of liberty, work for no pay, or boring and a waste of time. Half of those doing community service thought there were ways in which it could be improved. However, nearly 20 per cent thought there were no bad points about community service, mentioning the opportunity to do some kind of constructive work, the opportunity to learn new skills and gain experience, meeting others, the fact that it was something to do or somewhere to go, or that it was simply enjoyable.

Getting through the order and breaches (Chapter 5)

One-third of the sample admitted to further offending during their order; this was more likely for young offenders. Most had discussed this with their supervising officer; it is not possible to say from the survey what action probation officers were taking as a result.

Nine out of ten respondents thought it very likely that they would complete their order. However, nearly one-fifth of the whole sample had been warned that their probation officers were considering taking breach action. Those under 21 were more likely to have been warned. For three-quarters of those warned about breach, the reason was repeated failure to attend probation supervision sessions. Only six per cent had actually been breached, more than one-third of whom were in the 16 to 20 age group.

Attitudes towards and factors related to offending (Chapter 5)

For those with previous convictions the most common reason given for starting to offend (especially for young offenders) was peer pressure. Other common reasons were need for money or 'things', boredom, unemployment, problems at home, or stupidity or lack of thought.

Peer pressure was much less likely to be claimed as a reason for committing the *current* offence. Needing money/'things' was mentioned by 28 per cent of respondents. The second most popular reason was the influence of alcohol – a common response for those aged over 35.

Almost half of the sample said that the prospect of a community sentence would be a deterrent to reoffending. Three–quarters of the sample said that possibility of being sent to prison would stop them committing an offence. The most common reason given for probation helping to stop further offending was that probation helped you to understand why you had committed an offence.

Family and friends (Chapter 5)

About two-fifths of respondents said that a member of their family had been convicted of a criminal offence. In about three–quarters of cases, the family member was a brother/sister, and in a third of cases a parent was mentioned.

A number of family members had served a prison sentence. Most of those who had been imprisoned were close family; nearly two-thirds were siblings, and more than a third were parents.

Almost three-quarters of the sample said that they had friends who had been in trouble with the law. For those aged 16 to 20, the proportion was almost 90 per cent.

In nine out of ten cases respondents' families were aware that the respondent was on probation. Over a quarter of respondents said that their family did not care, a similar proportion said that their family thought that probation was good for them, 15 per cent said their family felt they were lucky not to be in prison, and the same percentage reported that their family was shocked and disgusted.

Eighty-five per cent of respondents said that their friends knew they were on probation; half of these reported that their friends did not care.

Conclusion (Chapter 6)

It is possible that those most critical of probation were not included in the survey. Nevertheless, the survey provides insight into the impact that probation makes on offenders. The probation service is viewed favourably by most of those it supervises, and is working to achieve its formal aims and objectives. Probationers' relationships with their supervisors are generally very positive. A majority of probationers think that probation has helped them to understand their offending behaviour and will help them to stay out of trouble. There is evidence also of a punitive effect, in that orders are restrictive of liberty.

1 Introduction

The Probation of Offenders Act 1907 officially established the probation service as we know it; the service has, therefore, been around for almost 100 years. During that time fashions in probation work have come and gone, types and levels of offending have changed, the number of probation officers and the scope of what the service does have grown considerably. It is timely to consider what goes on in the course of a probation order, what the offenders who are supervised think of it, and just how effective probation is.

Since the late eighties a higher proportion of serious offenders have been sentenced to probation orders – in 1985 only 30 per cent of those commencing probation had had experience of custody, whereas by 1993 this had increased to 43 per cent (Home Office, 1994). For the past ten years more than 40,000 offenders annually have commenced a probation order, while the combination order (introduced as part of the Criminal Justice Act 1991) within two years was dealing with more than 12,000 offenders. Public agencies have been subjected to considerable pressure to demonstrate effectiveness in the use of their resources, while at the same time these resources have been cut. Such factors have had – and continue to have – implications for the probation service, one of the most significant of which was the introduction of National Standards for the Supervision of Offenders in the Community in 1992 (Home Office, 1992). The National Standards generally emphasised consistency of practice in an effort to minimise the wide diversity of practice which was characteristic of probation work.

At the same time as the developments just noted, there were a series of other changes – some originating in the probation service itself and some deriving from the Home Office – which have made the service more accountable and have led it towards a rather more controlling approach to dealing with offenders (see Mair, 1996). It should be noted that this has not been achieved without a good deal of agonising on the part of probation officers who have worried about 'the end of probation as we know it'. For a brief period in the late eighties and early nineties, the service was encouraged to believe that it was to play a more important role in dealing with offenders, and that resources would be forthcoming to permit this. By 1994, however, the service saw itself as being increasingly marginalised. The Green Paper *Strengthening Punishment in the Community* (Home Office

1995a), the proposals to change the nature of probation training, and the introduction of curfew orders with electronic monitoring have all been received with some scepticism by probation officers.

The National Standards for probation orders set out clearly three statutory purposes of probation supervision: to secure the rehabilitation of the offender; to protect the public from harm; and to prevent further offending. Within the professional relationship which probation officers are expected to establish with their offenders, four specific objectives were listed in the Standards.[1] These were:

- securing the offender's co-operation and compliance with the probation order and enforcing its aims

- challenging the offender to accept responsibility for his or her crime and its consequences

- helping the offender to resolve personal difficulties linked with offending and to acquire new skills

- motivating and assisting the offender to become a responsible and law-abiding member of the community.

(Home Office, 1992)

Despite the growing pressure on the probation service to demonstrate its effectiveness in protecting the public and addressing offending behaviour, we still know very little about the nature of probation supervision or about those who receive such supervision. Recent work in relation to the development of performance indicators has demonstrated that sentencers have a fairly high opinion of the work of the service (May, 1995), but what about those offenders who are sentenced to probation or a combination order by the courts? They may be considered as 'customers' of probation services - though in a rather different way from the courts - and feedback from them may prove useful. How do offenders perceive a probation order, and what do they think of their probation officer? What are the personal characteristics of those who are supervised by probation officers, and what are their attitudes towards offending? A key objective of this study was to provide a fuller understanding of the backgrounds and current social and economic circumstances of offenders serving community orders. Such information would provide a context within which to examine offenders' experiences of probation, including their perceptions of its helpfulness in

---

1   It should be noted that these objectives have been revised in the new National Standards which were issued in 1995. (Home Office 1995b)

addressing problems and stopping further offending. This is not to argue that offenders' views are the only measure of effectiveness. However, the main alternative measure of effectiveness – reconviction rates – is known to have a number of limitations (see Lloyd, Mair and Hough, 1994) and there is clearly a need to develop a variety of approaches to examining the impact of community sentences (see Mair, 1991; Mair, et al., 1994).

Various studies have looked at the views of those on probation over the years (Bailey and Ward, 1992; Day, 1981; Ditton and Ford, 1994; Fielding, 1986; Mantle, 1995; Willis, 1986), but all of these have been small-scale and limited. In 1993, after considerable discussion and with the agreement of the Association of Chief Officers of Probation (ACOP) and the National Association of Probation Officers (NAPO), the then Home Office Research and Planning Unit commissioned Social and Community Planning Research (SCPR) to carry out a major survey of offenders undergoing probation supervision. It was decided to restrict the survey to those who had been sentenced to a probation order (with or without requirements) or combination order; to have included those with community service orders only would have greatly increased the already considerable difficulties of access to offenders.

The survey questionnaire was designed by SCPR in conjunction with the Home Office and the topics covered included background characteristics of the respondents, details of the offences and the orders, views and attitudes towards the orders and the probation officers, and attitudes towards offending. The survey took place in the first half of 1994.

This study reports the findings of the survey. Chapter 2 describes the methodology. Chapter 3 discusses the characteristics of the sample, and Chapters 4 and 5 discuss the results of the survey. Chapter 6, finally, attempts to assess the implications of this first major survey of offenders under probation supervision.

2 Methodology and fieldwork

This chapter summarises briefly the methodology used for the survey. Those who are interested in more detail are referred to the technical report (Dundon-Smith, Ghate and Hales, 1994).

Research design

It was planned to achieve a sample of 2,000 offenders in England and Wales, so that sub-groups of the sample could be examined. Assuming a response rate of up to 85 per cent this suggested an initial sample of about 2,400 offenders.

The survey covered offenders on a probation order or a combination order, including those with additional requirements. Only those who had completed at least three months of their order were included.

Before drafting the questionnaire SCPR visited two probation teams in South East London to interview a number of offenders and probation officers in an unstructured way. A pilot survey was then conducted in seven offices in four probation areas. Twenty-four offenders were interviewed, covering both sexes and a range of ages and types of order.

The final questionnaire was based largely on that used in the pilot. The average interview was expected to take approximately 50 minutes.

Sampling

The sample design was intended to give each current probation order an equal chance of selection. This type of sample design results in a sample which is representative of all those currently on probation.

The first stage of sampling was to select a number of probation areas in such a way that larger areas had a greater chance of inclusion. Initially, 24 of the then 55 probation areas in England and Wales were selected. Not all of these were able to participate, but it was agreed to proceed in 22 areas.

In the second stage of sampling a random sample of 150 offenders was selected from each area. This sample was drawn from the Home Office's Probation Index, a national statistical database of probation offenders and orders, because it was readily available and provided uniform coverage of the population. Unfortunately, because of difficulties in recording movements of offenders, they were not necessarily supervised at the offices identified on the Index. However, with assistance of the probation areas it was possible to give each interviewer a listing of their sample, including addresses and contact names.

The total issued sample was 3,299 offenders.

Fieldwork

The fieldwork was carried out between April and June 1994. In most areas there were four interviewers, with up to six in the larger areas. As far as possible it was the task of the interviewer, rather than probation staff, to introduce the survey to offenders. Interviews were conducted mainly at the general probation offices which were supervising each offender and if possible on the day of each offender's regular visit. In fact, nearly half of the interviews with respondents were carried out on a day when they had a session with their probation officer.

Ideally attempts to obtain interviews with offenders were to be pursued indefinitely. However, towards the end of the survey interviewers were told that after two broken appointments they should assume that they would be unlikely to obtain an interview with that offender. They should only make a further appointment if probation staff felt that there was a reasonable likelihood that the offender would keep the appointment. Nearly 97 per cent of the interviews were carried out within three appointments, of which 70 per cent were conducted on the first appointment. The average interview length was 52 minutes.

Non-response and the achieved sample

Of the issued sample of 3,299 offenders it was found that nearly 40 per cent could not be contacted. The main reasons for this were that they had been taken into custody, or their order had terminated, or they had been transferred to another area.

The effective sample, after subtracting those who could not be contacted, was 1,986. Of these 1,213 interviews were achieved, giving a response rate of 61 per cent. Only eight per cent of offenders refused to take part.

However, 27 per cent of respondents failed to keep an appointment either with the interviewer or with the probation officer when the interviewer was to be present to introduce the survey. In many cases this also implies a refusal to participate. It is possible that those who could not be interviewed will have had a more negative attitude to the probation service than those included, resulting in some bias in the sample. This should be remembered when considering the findings.

The response rate varied according to the size of probation areas. The highest response was generally achieved in the smallest areas, with a rate of 76 per cent in one such area. The lowest response (36%) was recorded in one of the London probation areas. One-third of sample members in London areas were either not available or broke their appointment, and in the London areas it tended to be more difficult to arrange appointments. It follows that the achieved sample over-represented the smallest probation areas and under-represented London.

In any sample survey there is a risk of bias. The achieved sample was compared with all the issued sample on a series of characteristics. This analysis showed that the sample did not appear to be strongly biased in terms of sex or age, though there was a slight under-representation of the two age groups 16–20 and 21–24 and a corresponding over-representation of those aged 30 and over.

The achieved sample also reflected the composition of the issued sample when comparing the type and length of the order – 84 per cent of the sample were on a probation order only, 12 per cent were on a combination order and four per cent were on probation and serving a separate community service order. The time elapsed on the order could also be expected to affect the ability of interviewers to achieve interviews. Those whose order began in the final quarter of 1993 are under-represented in the achieved sample. This is probably because records for these offenders would have had the least time to be brought up to date on the Probation Index.

Weighting

The sample was designed so that, to give a representative sample, the same number of offenders should be interviewed in each of the selected probation areas. However, this was not achieved. There were differences both in the percentages who could not be contacted and in the response rate from area to area. This meant that it was necessary to apply corrective weightings to the findings, so that, for example, the results from an area with a large sample did not disproportionately affect the overall results.

The difference between the weighted and non-weighted results is not generally significant when analysing the findings by age, sex, type and length of order.

A note on the tables

The tables in this report give weighted percentages and the actual numbers of cases on which the weighted percentages are based. The sex of two respondents was not recorded, nor was the age of one respondent. This means that, in the tables based on age and sex separately, the actual numbers do not total the achieved number of interviews, 1,213. However, the 'All' column in such tables is based on *all* respondents. There may also be other missing cases for some of the variables tabulated.

The sign * in the tables represents less than $1/2$ per cent but greater than zero.

3 Characteristics of the sample

Demographic characteristics

Table 3.1 shows the composition of the sample by type of order and sex, compared with official statistics of persons on probation at the end of 1993.

Table 3.1 Composition of the sample by type of order and sex

	Persons on probation on 31 December 1993	Survey sample
	%	%
Probation – males	73	71
Probation – females	16	17
Combination orders – males	10	11
Combination orders – females	1	2
n	46,302	1,209

Women on combination orders were over-represented in the sample, but the number involved was small (23). For the larger sections of the population the sample was representative in terms of sex and type of order.

The age distribution of male and female respondents was very similar, with just over 40 per cent of both groups falling into the 16 to 24 age range (43% of males and 45% of females, Table 3.2).

Table 3.2 Composition of the sample by age and sex

Age	Persons on probation on 31 December 1993		Survey	
	Males	Females	Males	Females
	%	%	%	%
16–20	21	17	21	20
21–24	25	22	22	25
25–29	21	24	19	17
30–39	21	26	23	28
40–49	9	9	11	7
50–59	3	2	3	3
60 and over	1	*	2	1
n			996	214

Statistical tests show that the sample was generally representative in terms of age, with a few exceptions. Males aged 40 to 49 and those over 60 were slightly over-represented, while females aged 25 to 29 were slightly under-represented.

The age distribution of probationers is similar to that found for prisoners in the National Prison Survey (NPS) of 1991 (Dodd and Hunter, 1992) where 40 per cent of prisoners were aged under 25 with five per cent aged 50 or over. However, in comparison with the general population of England and Wales, the probation sample (and the prison sample) is much younger. Census data for 1991 show that around one-fifth of males and females in the general population are aged between 16 and 24, while for the probation sample more than two-fifths of both groups fell into this age range (Table 3.3).[1] Given that we know that the peak age of known offending for males is between 15 and 18, and is 15 for females, this result is not surprising.

---

1 For the remainder of this chapter, unless otherwise noted, where comparisons are made to the prison sample, data have been taken from the National Prison Survey.

Table 3.3 Age and sex - comparison with general population England and Wales, ages 16 to 59 only.

	Census 1991		Survey	
Age	Male	Female	Male	Female
	%	%	%	%
16–24	22	22	43	45
25–29	13	14	20	17
30–39	24	24	23	28
40–49	23	23	11	8
50–59	18	18	3	3
n			983	213

The great majority of respondents were white (93%, compared with 95% of adults in the general population). Five per cent defined themselves as black and one per cent as Asian. Fewer than 20 females were from ethnic minorities. The NPS showed that a higher proportion of prisoners than probationers were from ethnic minorities; 82 per cent of prisoners were white, with 11 per cent black and four per cent Asian.

About half of the sample was single (52%), with one-third (33%) married or living together as married, and 16 per cent widowed, divorced or separated (this is almost exactly the same as in the NPS). For the general population, however, only 21 per cent were single and 65 per cent married or living together as married. Interestingly, probationers and prisoners aged 16 to 20 were far more likely to be married or living together as married than those in the population as a whole (19%, 17% and 3% respectively). The two offender groups were more likely to be separated or divorced than those in the general population, especially those in the 30 to 59 age range; and prisoners aged 40 or more were the group most likely to be single (see Table A.1 in the Appendix).

Nearly a quarter of all probationers lived alone, with the proportion increasing from 12 per cent for those under 21, to 41 per cent for those aged 50 or more (see Table A.2 in the Appendix). Nearly a third of female probationers were living alone with dependent children, compared with 14 per cent of both female prisoners and women of child-bearing age in the general population in 1993. The latter figure is estimated from the Census and from Social Trends (Central Statistical Office, 1994 and 1996). See Table A.3 in the Appendix.

In terms of employment, only 21 per cent were employed or self-employed (4% said that they were self-employed, and two-thirds of those had no-one working for them). Of those who were employed, 79 per cent were in manual occupations.

As Table 3.4 shows, young people were more likely to be out of work than older respondents, and older age groups were much more likely to be permanently sick or disabled. Forty-two per cent of females were looking after the home or family. According to Census data, 64 per cent of males aged 16 to 64 are in employment, as are 59 per cent of females aged 16 to 59; and prisoners were more likely to have been employed prior to imprisonment than probationers, with 51 per cent of NPS respondents saying that they had had a job.

Table 3.4 Employment by age and sex

	Male	Female	16–20	21–35	36 or more	All
	%	%	%	%	%	%
Employed	23	12	17	22	24	21
Signing on as unemployed	59	34	66	54	44	54
Looking after home or family	1	42	4	11	5	8
Permanently sick	11	7	1	9	21	10
Retired	1	0	0	0	3	1
Other	6	5	12	4	4	6
n	996	214	255	697	260	1,213

Education and childhood

A significant minority of respondents had spent time in some form of care before they were 16, with almost one-fifth having spent time in a residential children's home (one-third of them for more than three years) and 14 per cent having lived in a borstal or young offenders unit (Table 3.5). One-quarter of prisoners had been taken into care before the age of 16, but only two per cent of the general population (Bridgwood and Malbon, 1995).

Table 3.5 *Percentages of the sample spending time in care before the age of 16*

	Male	Female	16–20	21–35	36 or more	All
Living with a foster family	9	10	14	9	5	9
Living with an adopted family	3	4	2	4	4	3
Living in a residential children's home	18	20	22	21	9	19
Living in a borstal or young offenders unit	14	4	8	15	11	13
n	996	214	255	697	260	1,213

Overall, 68 per cent of the sample said that they had lived with both parents up to the age of 16 (when not in care in the case of those who had spent time in care). Around a fifth of probationers and prisoners had been brought up in a one-parent family (the comparable figure for prisoners was 19%). Women and those under the age of 21 were more likely to have lived with only one parent (28% of women compared with 20% of men; and 27% of those under 21 compared with 11% of those age 36 or over).

Forty-two per cent of the sample had left school under the age of 16, and 49 per cent left at age 16; for prisoners the comparable figures are 43 per cent and 46 per cent; while for the population as a whole they are 44 per cent and 33 per cent (Bridgwood and Malbon, 1995). One-fifth of female and 13 per cent of male respondents said that they had entered full-time further or higher education. While a wide range of examinations had been passed and technical qualifications awarded, on the whole the sample was not particularly well qualified. Of males 12 per cent had gained 'O' levels, four per cent 'A' levels and one per cent a university degree (see Table A.4 in the Appendix). The equivalent figures in the general population in 1992 were 19 per cent, 14 per cent and 11 per cent (Office of Population Censuses and Surveys, 1994).

For those with no qualifications, comparisons with prisoners and the population as a whole are interesting, as Table 3.6 shows.

Table 3.6 Percentages of probationers, prisoners, and the general population with no qualifications, by age and sex

	Probation	Prison	General population
16–20	52	52	23
21–24	47	46	16
25–29	42	41	18
30–39	52	34	28
40–49	50	41	41
50–59	47	48	53
60 or over	49	47	65
males	48	43	34
females	51	40	42
All	49	43	39

Those on probation are more likely to be unqualified than prisoners, who in turn are more likely to be unqualified than the population as a whole. There is not a great deal of variation according to age in the two offender groups, but for the general population older people are less well qualified than younger age groups.

Accommodation and finances

Most respondents rented their accommodation either from a local authority or housing association (70%). The corresponding figure for the general population is 25 per cent of households (Office of Population Censuses and Surveys, 1994). Although the figures are not strictly comparable, the latter being based on households, they almost certainly indicate a different pattern of accommodation for probationers compared with the general population.

Only seven per cent of probationers were renting a bedsit or living in bed and breakfast accommodation, a hostel or some form of temporary accommodation. Perhaps surprisingly, no difference by age in probationers' accommodation was apparent.

Given the levels of unemployment among the sample mentioned above, it is not surprising that two-thirds said that the main source of income for their household was state benefit. When asked whether they had problems with paying essential bills 19 per cent said 'always' and 22 per cent said 'sometimes'. Just over one-third (35%) said that they currently had problems with debt – with utility companies, banks or building societies, and mail order companies being most likely to be named. It is intriguing that 'someone else' (apart from a friend or relative) was, along with utility companies the most commonly mentioned as being owed money. As Table 3.7 shows, there were some differences in those who were owed money according to the age of the respondent, with the youngest age group being least likely to owe money on ordinary household bills, but most likely to owe money to the mysterious 'someone else'.

Table 3.7 Those to whom respondents owed money, by age
Base: Those owing money

	16–20	21–35	36 or over	All
	%	%	%	%
Bank, building society	11	26	40	25
Credit card	3	7	16	8
Mail order	23	22	13	20
Private loan	11	11	15	12
Landlord	9	20	14	17
Utilities	15	39	49	36
Family member	19	12	13	13
Friend	13	13	12	13
Someone else	52	36	19	36
Not answered	0	1	1	1
n	81	253	80	414

Only one-quarter of the probationers held a current licence to drive a car, compared with two-thirds of the general population (Department of Transport, 1995). See Table A.5 in the Appendix. The likelihood of having a licence increased with age, but the difference between offenders and the general population was apparent in all age groups. It is notable that male and female probationers were about equally likely to hold a driving licence, while in the general population men were more likely to have a licence. This may be partly explained by the fact that men are more likely to be convicted for driving offences and car theft and so lose their licence.

Health

Almost half of the sample (49%) said that they currently had or expected to have certain long-term health problems or disabilities listed on a show card (long-term was defined as for at least six months). In a recent survey of the health of prisoners (Bridgwood and Malbon, 1995), 48 per cent of male prisoners said that they had some form of long-standing illness or disability.

Table 3.8 shows the problems or disabilities mentioned by probationers and the percentages who mentioned them, broken down by age and sex. There are considerable differences between male and female respondents, and between young and old.

The Health Survey for England (Bennett et al., 1994) collects information on the health of adults through interviews, measurements and blood tests. It is difficult to compare the more objective data from that survey with the information collected in this study, however, probationers report long-term illness or disability more often than the Health Survey would suggest. For example, 69 per cent of male probationers aged between 45 and 64 reported a long-term illness or disability, compared with 46 per cent of males in the general population; and for males aged 16 to 44 the figures were 46 per cent for probationers and 26 per cent for the population as a whole.

Table 3.9 shows percentages of males aged 18 to 49 reporting long-term conditions, comparing probationers, prisoners and the general population (Bridgwood and Malbon, 1995). The categories of illness between the three surveys are not strictly comparable, but it is clear that the proportions of probationers and prisoners reporting long-term illness or disability are similar, and both are higher than in the general population.

Table 3.8 Health problems or disabilities lasting longer than six months by age and sex

	Male			Female			
	16–20	21–35	36 or over	16–20	21–35	36 or over	All
	%	%	%	%	%	%	%
Musculoskeletal system	11	16	32	8	13	27	18
Eye complaints	3	4	6	2	7	4	4
Ear complaints	2	3	3	0	2	3	2
Skin complaints	2	7	6	10	14	2	7
Respiratory system	15	15	12	16	17	16	15
Heart, blood pressure	2	2	14	9	6	10	5
Digestive system	1	5	9	5	12	7	6
Diabetes	0	1	2	0	3	2	1
Mental disorders, depression	5	15	17	5	16	33	14
Learning difficulties	2	5	2	0	2	0	3
Epilepsy	2	3	5	0	5	2	3
Other	3	6	5	1	7	16	5
No long-term health problem	66	53	37	57	49	33	51
n	211	567	218	44	129	41	1,213

Note: Percentages do not necessarily add to 100 as an offender may have more than one health problem.

Table 3.9 Percentages of males aged 18 to 49 reporting long-standing conditions: comparison between people on probation, prisoners and the general population

	Probation	Prisoners	General population
Musculoskeletal system	17	16	12
Respiratory system	14	15	8
Digestive system	5	5	3
Ear and eye complaints	6	4	3
Heart and circulatory system	4	3	3
Skin complaints	6	3	1
n	922	925	4,407

Probationers were asked if health problems limited the amount of paid work they could do, and almost one-third (30%) said that it did. Responses are shown in Table 3.10, where they are compared with limiting long-term illness in the general population (Office of Population Censuses and Surveys, 1995).

Table 3.10 Percentages reporting limiting long-term illness, comparing offenders on probation and the general population

Age	Probationers: percentage with illness lasting at least six months	Probationers: percentage where illness limits paid work	General Population: Self-reported limiting long-standing illness
16 to 44	47 (n=1,110)	29 (n=1,110)	13 (n=9,500)
45 to 64	72 (n=89)	46 (n=89)	29 (n=5,600)
All aged 16 to 64	49 (n=1,199)	30 (n=1,199)	19 (n=15,100)

It should be emphasised again that the definitions used in the two surveys are not identical, but it is clear that a larger proportion of those on probation than in the general population as a whole considered themselves to be affected by long-term illness. In addition, nearly five per cent of probationers said they were registered as disabled, compared with less than three per cent of the population as a whole (a statistically significant difference).

Drug and alcohol use

At the end of the interview part of the questionnaire, respondents were offered a short self-completion booklet which asked some questions about drug and alcohol use. It is a common claim that a considerable amount of offending is associated with the misuse of alcohol or drugs, and there is increasing evidence that a good deal of probation work is carried out with offenders who misuse drugs (see Nee and Sibbitt, 1993). Almost all of the sample agreed to complete the booklet (in only 32 cases was the booklet left blank or refused) and for most of these the booklet was completed without interviewer assistance (63%). The questions on drug use were the same as those asked in the 1992 British Crime Survey (Mott and Mirrlees–Black, 1995), and similar to those asked in the 1994 British Crime Survey (Ramsay and Percy, 1996). Results from the probationer sample will be compared with the results of these surveys where appropriate.

Around half (55%) of the sample had been offered drugs in the previous 12 months (see Table A.6 in the Appendix). Over three-quarters of males aged 16 to 20 had been offered drugs. Cannabis (mentioned by 49%), amphetamines (37%), LSD (27%), Ecstasy (25%)and Temazepam (22%) were the drugs most likely to have been offered. Heroin, cocaine, crack and methadone were mentioned by between 11 and 15 per cent of the sample, but were most often mentioned by those in the 21 to 35 age group. British Crime Survey (BCS) results for 1992 (this question was not asked in 1994) followed a similar pattern to the probation sample, but the percentages stating that they had been offered drugs were consistently lower (for example, only 50% of males aged 16 to 19 said they had been offered any drug in the previous 12 months). This is only to be expected as the probation sample consisted of convicted offenders while the BCS sample consisted of a sample of the general population, and it is likely that offenders will move in circles where drugs are available more often than other members of the general public.

Having been offered drugs, however, only gives a rough idea of the availability of drugs to the sample. Table 3.11 shows respondents' drug usage in the previous 12 months, broken down by age and sex.

Table 3.11 Percentages of offenders who had taken particular drugs in the past 12 months, by age and sex

	Male	Female	16-20	21-35	36 or more	All
Cannabis	45	29	56	47	16	42
Amphetamines	25	22	33	28	8	24
Temazepam	16	11	17	18	7	15
LSD	15	8	26	14	2	14
Ecstasy	13	8	22	13	1	12
Magic mushrooms	11	4	17	10	2	10
Heroin	9	8	4	12	3	8
Cocaine	9	4	11	9	4	8
Methadone	8	8	3	10	5	8
Crack	5	5	3	6	1	5
None of these drugs taken	40	53	29	37	70	42
Unanswered/ blank	10	13	8	11	11	10
n	996	214	255	697	260	1,213

The pattern of drugs taken is very similar to that of drugs offered: cannabis (42%) and amphetamines (24%) were by far the most popular, followed by Temazepam (15%), LSD (14%) and Ecstasy (12%), all drugs associated with youth culture. Those aged 21 to 35 were most likely to have used crack, heroin and methadone, while those aged 36 or over were least likely to have used drugs generally. On the whole, women were less likely to have taken drugs than men, although in the case of amphetamines, methadone, heroin and crack their usage was on a par with that of men. Table 3.12 compares drug use in the previous 12 months for the probation sample and BCS respondents in 1994.

Table 3.12 Percentages of males and females who had taken particular drugs in the last year, ages 16 to 29 only, compared with results from BCS 1994

	Males		Females		All	
	probation	BCS	probation	BCS	probation	BCS
Cannabis	57	25	39	16	54	20
Amphetamines	33	9	28	5	32	7
LSD	22	5	11	3	20	4
Magic mushrooms	15	4	6	1	13	3
Ecstasy	19	4	10	2	17	3
Temazepam	20	1	15	1	19	1
Cocaine	11	1	5	1	10	1
Crack	6	0	4	*	5	*
Methadone	9	*	9	*	9	*
Heroin	10	1	7	*	9	*
n	633	1,204	134	1,573	767	2,777

It is clear from the table that drug use is far more common among the probationers than BCS respondents; and while females in general were less likely to have used drugs than men, female probationers had used drugs more often than male BCS respondents (see Table A.7 in the Appendix for a comparison of male probationers and BCS respondents according to age).

When asked which drugs had ever been taken, patterns of usage increased considerably: use of Ecstasy, LSD, heroin and methadone doubled, while cocaine and crack use more than doubled. Almost one-quarter of those aged 21 to 35 claimed to have used cocaine and heroin at some time.

Respondents were asked about the various methods they had tried in taking drugs in the past 12 months and ever. Smoking/sniffing /inhaling was by far the most common method (43% had tried this in the past 12 months), followed by swallowing/eating/drinking (29%), and by injecting (10%). Women were just as likely as men to have injected, and this method was most common for the 21 to 35 age group. BCS data for 1992 suggested that fewer than 0.5 per cent of the general population had ever injected drugs.

The final two questions on the booklet covered drinking habits. Unfortunately it has not proved possible to compare the responses with those from any other surveys of drinking patterns. However, the results are interesting in themselves.

Respondents were offered a series of statements describing drinking patterns and were asked to tick every box which applied to them. Table 3.13 shows responses to this question.

Only 14 per cent said that they never drank, although a further 34 per cent claimed that they only drank rarely; women were more likely to fall into these categories than men. Those aged 36 or over were most likely to say that they drank most days of the week, whereas young offenders seemed to be more likely to drink heavily at weekends. Even taking account of the fact that individuals may inflate or deflate their drinking habits for reasons of their own, there would appear to be at least 10 per cent of the sample who had a drink problem (taking the final four responses as an indicator of this).

The final question asked about current drinking habits compared with those just before being put on probation. Whether or not it was due to probation, 30 per cent of respondents said that they drank a lot more before being put on probation than they drank at the time of the interview; on the other hand, seven per cent said they drank a lot less prior to being on probation!

Table 3.13 Drinking habits by age and sex - percentages of offenders agreeing with given statements

	Male	Female	16–20	21–35	36 or more	All
I never drink alcohol	12	22	10	15	16	14
I very rarely drink alcohol	32	43	39	35	28	34
I usually drink at weekends, but notin the week	31	26	33	30	25	30
I drink most days of the week	16	4	13	11	20	13
I usually drink a lot at weekends	13	6	14	13	6	12
I usually stop drinking before I get drunk	19	13	17	18	19	18
I usually get drunk at least once a week	11	7	12	12	6	10
I usually get drunk more than once a week	7	2	9	6	4	6
There have been times when I have felt that I was unable to stop drinking	10	5	8	10	10	9
I sometimes go on drinking binges	16	8	13	15	12	14
I have had a drink first thing in the morning to steady my nerves or to get rid of a hangover	7	2	6	7	6	7
I have found that my hands were shaking in the morning after drinking the previous night	10	6	8	11	8	9
Unanswered/ blank	3	3	3	3	3	3
n	996	214	255	697	260	1,213

Current sentence and offence

As mentioned in Chapter 2, 84 per cent of the sample were currently on a probation order only; 12 per cent were on a combination order; while four per cent were on a probation order and also serving a separate community service order. Those in the 16 to 20 age group were almost twice as likely to be serving a combination order as those aged 36 or over (14% compared with 8%). Most orders were for between 13 and 24 months (55%), with just over one-third for 7 to 12 months. In the case of combination orders, the community service element lasts between 40 and 100 hours; many of our respondents, however, seemed to be unclear about the length of their community service element with more than half claiming that this was for more than 100 hours.

For just over half of the respondents (51%) it was their first time on probation; for women (65%) and young offenders (67%) this was more likely to be the case than for men and older offenders. For those who had been on probation before, most (57%) had had two probation orders (including the current one) while one-quarter had had three probation orders.

Patterns of offending generally differ according to gender and age and the sample proved to be no exception (Table 3.14).

Table 3.14 Current offence by age and sex

	Male	Female	16-20	21-24	25-29	30-39	40 or older	All
	%	%	%	%	%	%	%	%
Violence	19	16	19	21	18	17	18	19
Sexual	5	0	3	1	4	3	11	4
Burglary	23	6	30	24	22	17	4	20
Robbery	2	4	5	1	1	2	1	2
Car theft/theft from car	12	3	23	12	10	4	0	10
Other theft/ handling	13	35	15	19	15	20	16	17
Fraud, forgery, deception	7	29	5	8	14	15	13	11
Criminal damage	6	5	9	8	3	5	4	6
Drink-driving	14	4	1	6	11	20	27	12
Other driving	14	3	17	13	10	11	7	12
Drugs-related	6	5	4	10	6	4	5	6
Other	4	5	6	5	4	3	4	4
n	993	213	255	277	233	266	177	1,208

Men were far more likely to have been convicted of burglary, driving offences, and theft of, or from, cars than women; while women were much more likely than men to have been convicted of theft or handling offences and fraud or forgery. Burglary was less common as age increased, as was car theft; on the other hand, drink driving offences were far more common among older age groups. Not surprisingly, compared with prisoners, the probation sample had been convicted of less serious offences: only two per cent of probationers had been convicted of robbery, for example, compared with 13 per cent of prisoners; for sexual offences the respective figures were four per cent and nine per cent; and for thefts and fraud they were 38 per cent and 13 per cent.

Two-thirds of respondents had been sentenced in the magistrates' courts, 31 per cent in the Crown Court, and two per cent in the Youth Court. Women were rather more likely than men to have been sentenced in the Crown Court (38% compared with 30%), although there was no evidence that their offences were more serious than those committed by men.

Previous criminal history

Respondents were asked whether they had ever been convicted of an offence apart from the one which led to their current order; 82 per cent said they had been previously convicted (the figure for no previous convictions in the 1993 *Probation Statistics* for all probation orders is 19%). Women were more likely to be first offenders than men (36% compared with 13%), and, as might be expected, older offenders were more likely than young offenders to have been convicted before.

Male respondents were more likely than females to have begun their criminal career below the age of 18: 76 per cent of males said that they were first convicted of an offence at the age of 18 or less, while this was the case for 59 per cent of females. More than a quarter of those aged 36+ had been older than 25 when first convicted.

Respondents were asked about the first offence for which they were convicted (see Table A.8 in the Appendix for a breakdown by age and sex), and Table 3.15 compares these offences with the current offence.

Table 3.15 Offence at first conviction and current offence

	At first conviction	Current conviction (those with previous convictions)	Current conviction (those with no previous convictions)
	%	%	%
Violence	11	19	17
Sexual	1	3	9
Burglary	25	22	13
Robbery	3	2	3
Car theft/ theft from car	12	11	7
Other theft/ handling	24	18	13
Fraud, forgery, deception	5	9	19
Criminal damage	11	6	5
Drink-driving	6	12	12
Other driving	11	13	6
Drugs-related	2	6	6
Other	10	4	4
n	989	989	217

Burglary, theft and criminal damage together made up 60 per cent of the offences for which respondents were first convicted; in the case of current offences, however, these only made up 45 per cent of offences where there were previous convictions, and 31 per cent where the current offence was the first offence. Violence, fraud or forgery and drink driving offences, on the other hand, tended not to be first offences (they made up 22%), but they did make up 41 per cent of current offences where there were previous convictions, and 48 per cent where the current offence was a first one. It is not easy to discern any patterns here, for example there is little evidence of escalation between the first convicted offences and the current ones. It is interesting, however, that current offences for first offenders were considerably different from the first convicted offences for those with previous convictions. The higher proportion of fraud and forgery offences amongst those with no previous convictions may be partly explained by the high proportion of women in this group – women in the sample were much more likely to be convicted for these offences. The low proportion of burglary offences may similarly be explained – women were less likely to be convicted for burglary.

The most common sentence for the first offence was a fine, which half of those who had been convicted previously received. Women were more likely to have been conditionally discharged than men (24% compared with 14%), and young offenders were three times more likely than those aged 36 or over to have begun with a conditional discharge (29% against 9%). Probation was the second most common first sentence for older offenders (18%), but fourth most common for those aged 16 to 20 (11%).

Everyone was asked if they had committed an offence prior to their first conviction for which they had not been caught and 46 per cent admitted that they had. The most common offences which had been committed prior to the first conviction were theft or handling (42%), burglary (34%) and car theft or theft from a car (25%). Again, there were differences according to the age and sex of respondents (see Table A.9 in the Appendix).

Summary

Overall the sample of probationers was predominantly young, male and unemployed – which very much conforms to the stereotype of offenders, but is not at all similar to the general population where the average age is higher, the unemployment rate is lower and the balance between males and females is much closer. Roughly one in five of the sample had spent time in care, compared with only one in fifty of the population as a whole, and a similar proportion had been brought up in one-parent families; they were not well qualified educationally and more than 90 per cent had left school by the age of 16 compared with around three-quarters of the general population. There were also major differences in marital status with just over half of the probationers being single whereas this was the case for only one in five of the overall population (where the average age is higher). Interestingly, however, probationers aged 16 to 20 were about six times more likely to be married or living as married than their counterparts in the general population.

Given these general characteristics, it is perhaps not surprising that the sample was heavily dependent upon state benefits, had difficulty in paying bills and, for the most part, lived in rented accommodation. Compared with the population as a whole, their health was poor. A significant minority appear to have been problem drinkers, and compared with the population as a whole they were much more likely to have used drugs.

The great majority of respondents had previously been convicted. Their first official offence tended to be burglary, theft or damage – offences which are simple to commit and where no real expertise is required – and the first sentence tended to be a fine. Almost half of the sample admitted to having committed an offence before their first conviction.

In general, probationers appear to have a variety of needs and problems. Their characteristics are, on the whole, similar to those in custody – with both groups being very different from the overall population. Irrespective of how these characteristics are related to offending, the poverty and deprivation exhibited by those on probation is an important factor which is likely to have implications for supervision and should not be forgotten or dismissed.

4 Starting an order, supervision and supervisors

This chapter is the first of two which discuss the findings of the survey. It focuses on the details of the order and how it was seen to be put into practice by respondents. It also looks at the content of supervision and views on probation and probation officers.

Beginning the current order

Guidelines for what should happen at the commencement of a probation order are set out in the National Standards for Probation Orders (Home Office, 1992)[1]. At the initial appointment the officer should give the offender written information about what it means to be on probation, explain this to the offender, if possible give the offender a copy of the order and ask him/her to sign it, and confirm that he/she has agreed to the order. Eighty-five per cent of respondents said that they had been given a copy of their probation order to sign when they first started supervision; only two per cent said that this had not happened, while the remaining 13 per cent said that they could not remember or did not know. (It may be worth noting that this group had not been on probation significantly longer than those who did remember.) An even higher percentage – 93 per cent – said that their probation officer had made sure that they agreed to the order (again, most of the remainder could not remember). More than three-quarters (78%) said that they had been given a leaflet explaining what it meant to be on probation; 12 per cent said they had not been given any written information and 10 per cent could not remember. Ninety-four per cent said that they had been told by their probation officer what would happen in the event of a breach of the order.

Similar standards govern the commencement of a community service order, and the 162 respondents in the sample who were on a combination order were asked about their experiences. Seventy-nine per cent said that they

---

1   Unless otherwise noted, all references to the National Standards are to the 1992 version as this was the edition in operation at the time of the survey. The 1995 Standards cover the same issues as the first edition, but introduce tighter guidelines in some areas of work.

had been asked to sign a copy of the community service order, with only two per cent saying this had not occurred. Eighty-eight per cent said that the probation officer had checked that they agreed to the order, while 77 per cent said that they had been given written information about community service (12% said that they had not received any such information). And 94 per cent stated that their probation officer had informed them of what would happen if the order was breached. In most cases (71%), the community service order was not held by the same probation officer who held the probation order, but by a specialist in community service.

The 1992 National Standards for Probation Orders also stated that wherever possible within two weeks of sentence a supervision plan should be drawn up in consultation with the offender. This should be agreed with the offender, signed by him/her, a copy given to the offender, and the plan reviewed at least every three months. Two-thirds of respondents said that a supervision plan had been drawn up, 19 per cent said that this had not happened and 15 per cent could not remember.

For those cases where a plan had been put together, three-quarters said that their probation officer had asked what they thought should go into the plan, with the remainder equally split between those who said they had not been asked and those who could not remember. The great majority had agreed with what finally went into the plan, with only two per cent stating that they had not agreed with its contents. Three-quarters had been asked to sign the supervision plan (most of the remainder could not remember), and 61 per cent said they had been given a copy of the plan to keep. The pattern of use of supervision plans is shown in Table 4.1.

Overall, it is clear that while the majority of probation officers appear to be adhering to the National Standards, a significant minority are not doing so. In the case of supervision plans, nearly 20 per cent of all respondents said that a plan was not drawn up and 15 per cent could not remember or did not answer. Of those who said that a plan was drawn up 22 per cent said they were not given the plan, and 18 per cent could not remember or did not answer. It would be sensible to investigate further the reasons for this failure to adhere to the Standards – particularly as the revised Standards are more demanding than the first version.

Table 4.1 The use of supervision plans

	Supervision plan drawn up?	PO asked offender what should go in plan?	Offender agreed what went in plan?	Offender signed plan?	Offender given plan?
	Base: All	Base: Offenders stating that a supervision plan was drawn up			
	%	%	%	%	%
Yes	66	76	94	76	61
No	19	13	2	6	22
Can't remember/ not answered	15	11	5	19	18
n	1,213	810	810	810	810

Basic details of the current probation order

Half of the sample (51%) had their first supervision session with a probation officer within the same week as the court passed sentence; just over a quarter said that their first session was the following week, 11 per cent said that it was two weeks later, and seven per cent that it was more than two weeks later. The National Standards specify that the initial appointment should be arranged 'whenever possible' within five working days of the making of the order. It therefore looks as if at a minimum one in five offenders is not being seen within the guidelines. It should be noted that this is interpreting the findings favourably to the probation service; it is quite likely that more than half of those who said that their first session was the following week in fact saw their probation officer more than five days after the order was made, which could mean that more than one-third of orders did not comply with the National Standard.

Almost one-third (30%) of respondents were being supervised by a different probation officer from the one who was seen at the first supervision session.

Of these, the majority (69%) had had only two probation officers including their current one; 20 per cent claimed to have had three officers, and a surprising nine per cent said that they had had four or more. Those on combination orders or with additional requirements were no more likely to have had many probation officers than those on a straight probation order. For those who had had more than one supervising officer 80 per cent said that they had been supervised by him/her for one month or more.

Very few respondents (about one per cent) had asked to change their supervising officer since starting their order. Where the supervising officer had changed this was usually because he/she had left or changed jobs (44%) or the offender had moved to a different area (26%). More than nine out of ten respondents did, however, feel that those on probation should have the right to ask for a change of officer.

All respondents were asked whether their probation officer was a man or a woman: in 59 per cent of cases it was a woman and in 41 per cent it was a man (at the end of 1993, *Probation Statistics* showed 51% of maingrade officers as female). Fifty-six per cent of male offenders and 73 per cent of female offenders were supervised by female probation officers. Respondents were asked about their preference for male or female officers: for those being supervised by females only one per cent of male or female offenders said that they would prefer a male officer; and for those being supervised by males four per cent of male offenders and seven per cent of female offenders said that they would prefer to be supervised by a female officer. Both male and female offenders were more likely to be happy with female officers than with males.

The National Standards for Probation Orders suggested that, where practicable, in the first three months of the order an offender should be seen by his/her supervising officer on 12 occasions. This seems to have been followed for most cases in the sample: 83 per cent said that they were seen about once a week when they started on their probation order. There was an age difference, however: almost nine out of ten young offenders were seen weekly compared to three-quarters of those aged 36 or over. Just over a tenth (12 per cent) said that they were seen once a fortnight at the start of their order.

At the time of the survey, 40 per cent of respondents were being seen once a fortnight and 26 per cent once a month; only 18 per cent were being seen once a week, although again young offenders were most likely to fall into this group - 28 per cent of 16- to 20-year-olds said that they had a session with their supervising officer once a week, compared to 17 per cent of those aged 21 to 35 and 13 per cent of those aged 36 or more. This difference was not simply a consequence of the younger offenders being near to the start of their orders. However, session lengths were shorter for those under 21 and longer for those aged 40 or over, as Table 4.2 shows.

Table 4.2 Length of recent supervision sessions, by age of respondent

	16-20	21-24	25-29	30-39	40+	All
	%	%	%	%	%	%
About half an hour	49	45	40	42	35	42
30 minutes to 1 hour	34	37	39	36	47	38
Over 1 hour, less than 2	4	7	9	10	7	8
More than 2 hours	1	1	1	1	2	1
Varies	5	3	7	4	5	5
Other	8	8	7	7	4	7
n	255	278	235	267	177	1,213

Further analysis found that the length of session was not related to the length of the order, the stage of the order or the offence (those convicted of sex offences did tend to have longer sessions, but those aged 36 or over were more likely to have been convicted of such an offence). Those factors which were associated with session length were also related to age (for example, whether the offender was married, responsible for accommodation).

Overall, then, it looks as if sessions tended to be shorter but more frequent for those under 21, although the reasons for this are open to speculation.

The content of supervision

What is discussed in a session with a probation officer? Respondents were shown a list of subjects and asked which of them had been discussed in the latest session and which had been discussed in previous sessions. Offending behaviour was the most commonly discussed topic in previous sessions – 'why I committed the offence' was mentioned by 63 per cent of respondents. This indicates that officers are acting on the requirement in National Standards to challenge offenders to accept responsibility for their behaviour. The most commonly discussed subject in the most recent session was employment (42% – see Table A.10 in the Appendix); this was also commonly discussed at previous sessions (56%). Not surprisingly, topics were less likely to be discussed at the most recent session than to have been discussed in previous sessions, although the pattern (allowing for age and sex) was similar for both. Table 4.3 shows the topics discussed in previous sessions according to age and sex.

Female respondents were less likely than males to have discussed such subjects as the use of drugs or alcohol, employment, how their offence affected other people, and the constructive use of leisure time. On the other hand, they were rather more likely to discuss health problems and possibly also personal problems and problems with their family (though these last two differences were not statistically significant). This seems to point fairly clearly to a stereotypical view of females – although it may be grounded in a correct interpretation of the issues which confront them. For example, as was shown in the previous chapter, women were less likely than men to have used drugs and were less likely to be seeking work.

On the whole, young offenders were more likely than older offenders to have discussed most of the topics suggested; only on health and the consumption of alcohol was this pattern reversed. Chapter 3 showed that health problems were less common for young respondents, and that their alcohol use was less than that for older offenders, and tended to be concentrated at weekends. Taking drugs was discussed most by 21- to 24-year-olds; again this reflects the pattern of drug use.

As might be expected, there were relationships between the topics discussed at sessions and the characteristics of offenders: for example, problems with money were more likely to have been discussed if the respondent had stated that he/she was currently in debt; employment was discussed if the respondent was unemployed; taking drugs and alcohol consumption were discussed if the offender was a drug user or a heavy drinker. This confirms that probation officers are focusing on the problems which are likely to be associated with offending.

For the most part, other matters tended not to be discussed during sessions; only one-third of respondents mentioned other topics which they had talked about. The most commonly mentioned of these other topics was 'daily problems/everyday things' (14%), followed by hobbies/leisure activities (4%), past life events (4%) and court cases/legal actions (3%).

Table 4.3 Topics discussed in previous sessions with the probation officer, by age and sex of respondent - percentages mentioning particular topics

	Male	Female	16–20	21–24	25–29	30–39	40 or more	All
Things to do in spare time to keep out of trouble	56	40	62	61	50	49	38	53
Problems about where I live	52	50	54	56	48	55	42	52
Problems with money/debts	54	56	55	60	50	58	46	54
Employment	60	40	64	65	54	51	41	56
Problems with family	53	56	56	52	51	59	44	53
Personal problems	56	59	55	59	54	58	53	56
Why I committed the offence	64	60	72	67	56	61	58	63
How my offence affected other people	44	32	42	50	38	39	39	42
Taking drugs	34	23	35	42	32	31	14	32
Consumption of alcohol	44	22	31	41	40	46	43	40
Problems with my health	33	44	24	36	35	37	46	35
n	982	211	251	276	233	262	173	1,195

One of the major changes in probation work over the last 20 years has been a decrease in one-to-one counselling and an increase in group work of various kinds. Respondents were shown a list of projects/programmes and asked whether they had attended any of these since they had begun their probation order; in all, 40 per cent said that they had attended at least one of the projects listed. The most commonly used projects were alcohol management and counselling groups with 30 per cent of those attending groups stating that they attended such a programme; the least likely to be used were art or drama courses (attendance at specialist groups will be dependent to a considerable degree upon the local availability of groups and at the present time art/drama groups are not widely available in probation services). Of those attending groups women were more likely than men to attend a training/employment unit (32% compared to 20%). This may be a reflection of the fact that a lower proportion of women than men were employed; the data available does not allow further exploration of possible reasons, such as the content of schemes. Women were much less likely to attend an alcohol group (12% compared to 33%), and no women had attended a sex offenders group or a motor project. Four out ten women attending groups had attended a women's group.

Table 4.4 shows the programmes attended by respondents broken down by age group, and it is notable that younger offenders were more likely to have attended probation centres, motor projects and staying out of trouble courses than the oldest age groups. Older offenders, however, were more likely to have attended an alcohol group, and those in their twenties were more likely to have attended a drugs group.[2] Again, there is evidence of effective targeting here: those attending motor projects were more likely to have been convicted of car theft; and those attending drug/alcohol groups were those most likely to be heavy drinkers or drug users.

Besides the programmes specified, offenders on probation may be encouraged to contact various other organisations or agencies for help with their problems. Sixty-two per cent of the sample said that they had contacted such organisations, most commonly those which offered help with social and housing benefits (37% of all those who had contacted such agencies), and job training and work (34%). Women were less likely to have contacted agencies for help with employment, but more likely to have contacted Social Services than men. Help with health problems was more likely to have been sought by older respondents than young offenders, as was help with addiction to alcohol. On the other hand, young offenders tended to have sought help more often than older age groups for job training and work (see Table A.11 in the Appendix). In most cases, respondents said that their probation officer had suggested they contact such agencies rather than that they had been specified by the court as part of the order.

2　Respondents were asked whether they had attended programmes as a result of referral by their probation officer or whether as a result of an added condition of their order. There appears to have been some confusion on the part of the respondents, as, according to their responses, every programme was more likely to have been attended as a result of probation officer referral or advice. In the case at least of probation centres, motor projects and sex offender groups this seems unlikely.

Attendance at various other groups had been suggested by probation officers in a handful of cases, such as general self-help groups, an education course, or some form of psychiatric or psychotherapeutic counselling.

Table 4.4 Programmes attended by probationers by age group - percentages mentioning specified programmes

Base: those attending groups

	Male	Female	16–20	21–24	25–29	30–39	40 or more	All
A training or employment unit	20	32	28	20	21	21	19	22
A probation day centre	25	25	32	32	27	20	12	25
An art or drama project	3	0	1	3	4	1	2	2
A women's group	0	41	1	9	5	3	6	5
A probation staying out of trouble group	12	9	15	16	16	6	5	11
An alcohol management and counselling group	33	12	10	22	29	44	47	30
A sex offenders group	4	0	1	1	4	4	9	4
A drugs management group	14	17	7	20	22	15	5	14
A probation motor project	12	0	25	12	4	7	7	11
n	430	63	91	124	91	104	84	494

A significant minority of respondents said that their probation officer had given them help or advice with various money matters: 38 per cent said they had been helped with managing money, a similar percentage said they had been helped with meeting their expenses and paying bills, and 33 per cent said they had been helped with claiming social security benefits. In each case, women were more likely than men to have been given such help, even though women were no more likely than men to be having problems with debt. Those who did have problems with debt were slightly more likely to have been advised on one or more of these money matters – 58 per cent of them had been advised compared with 49 per cent of those not in debt. However 42 per cent of probationers with debt problems said they had not been given help or advice on any of these topics.

Despite the range of subjects which had been discussed or upon which advice had been offered, 14 per cent of the sample said that there were other things which they would have liked help with but their probation officer had not been able to offer or succeed in supplying. Of this group, the most commonly mentioned kind of help/advice concerned general problems (37%); however, 29 per cent mentioned help with accommodation, 12 per cent mentioned help with paying off debts, and nine per cent mentioned help with finding work.

To summarise this section briefly: during the course of supervision a wide range of programmes and agencies are used and topics discussed; these differ according to whether offenders are male or female and are also associated with problems presented by the offenders. There is a focus on discussing offending behaviour at supervision sessions and evidence that specific problems are being tackled during the course of supervision.

Views of and attitudes towards probation and probation officers

All respondents were asked why they thought they had been given a probation or combination order by the court rather than another sentence. The most common response (27%) was that the court had wanted the offender to benefit from the services available while on probation. The next most common (15%) was the perhaps more cynical point that it was because the offender had had a good lawyer or a positive pre-sentence report. Other common responses were that it was to give the respondent a chance (or a last chance) to prove him/herself; that it was a result of physical, emotional or mental health problems; and that it was a minor offence which did not deserve prison (see Table A.12 in the Appendix).

Interestingly, no-one mentioned that they had been given their current sentence in order to stop them reoffending. Women were more likely than men to feel that they had been given their sentence because of the effects of other sentences on the respondent's family/children; and older respondents were more likely than younger ones to see their sentence as a response to health problems.

By far the most popular 'good point' about being on probation was that it gave offenders access to someone independent to talk to about problems (54%); related to this point, a third of respondents mentioned getting practical help or advice with specific problems as a good thing. A further 19 per cent said that being helped to keep out of trouble and avoid offending was a good point about probation, while 15 per cent were rather more pragmatic and saw probation as good because it only involved a minor restriction on their liberty. There were few differences apparent according to age, although getting help with alcohol problems was mentioned far more often by older offenders (8% of those aged 36 or over compared with 2% of those aged 16 to 20). Table 4.5 sets out the good points of being on probation according to the sex of the respondent.

It is noticeable that, on the whole, female respondents tended to view the good points of probation as relating to their personal problems: they were more likely than men to mention such things as having someone to talk to, getting help with personal relationships, and the like. Fewer than one in ten probationers could not find a good point to mention.

As for the bad points about probation, the first thing to emphasise is that 54 per cent of the sample did not mention any at all. The most commonly mentioned bad point was the time taken to attend supervision sessions (24%), followed by the inconvenience of travelling to attend (7%). Only four per cent said that probation was a waste of time (see Table A.13 in the Appendix).

The great majority of respondents thought that their current probation order was either fairly or extremely useful (87%). As Table 4.6 shows, older offenders were more likely to see their orders as extremely useful. Further analysis shows that those whose main income was benefit, those not in work and those who had never taken drugs were more likely to rate their order as useful.

When asked for the reasons for their view of their order, respondents tended to repeat what they had stated as being the good or bad points points about probation.

Table 4.5 The good points of probation, by sex of respondent
Multiple responses possible

	Male	Female	All
	%	%	%
Having someone independent to talk to	53	61	54
Getting practical help and advice	32	37	33
Being helped to keep out of trouble	20	14	19
Minor restriction on liberty	16	9	15
To help understand offending behaviour	9	6	8
Something to do/gets you out of the house	4	3	4
Help with drinking problems	4	1	4
Having self-confidence boosted/ having someone who is interested	4	1	3
Help with personal/ relationship problems	3	6	3
Groups and activities	3	5	3
Help with drug problems	2	2	2
Friendliness of probation staff/ being treated with respect	2	3	2
No good points mentioned	9	6	9
n	996	214	1,213

Table 4.6 Usefulness of current order, by age and sex of respondent

	Male	Female	16–20	21–35	36 or more	All
	%	%	%	%	%	%
Extremely useful	46	52	40	46	55	47
Fairly useful	41	37	47	41	34	41
Not very useful	5	3	6	5	4	5
No use at all	6	5	6	7	5	6
Can't say/not applicable	2	3	2	1	2	2
n	996	214	255	697	260	1,213

Such positive views of probation were confirmed when all respondents were shown a card with five statements on it about being on probation. Table 4.7 shows how far respondents agreed or disagreed with these statements.

More than 60 per cent of the sample agreed strongly with the first two – rather general statements – about probation officers being able to help people. Interestingly, slightly less than half of the black respondents agreed strongly with these statements. Respondents were less likely to agree strongly with the more specific statements. Just over half of the sample agreed strongly that their probation officer helped them to come to terms with events in the past. Fewer than half, however, agreed strongly that being on probation kept them out of trouble, while just over one-third agreed strongly that being on probation would help them to stop offending altogether. Overall, those aged 36 or over, those on probation for the firsttime, and those who had not changed probation officer tended to be more positive than other groups about being on probation. Perhaps not surprisingly, offenders with more negative characteristics themselves (such as taking drugs, still offending, heavy drinking, debt, unsettled childhoods) tended to have more negative views of probation.

Using another show card respondents were asked how far they agreed or disagreed with ten statements as they related to their own probation officer. Table 4.8 sets out the responses.

Table 4.7 Views about being on probation
Row percentages
(n=1,213)

	Agree strongly	Agree slightly	Neither agree nor disagree	Disagree slightly	Disagree strongly	Don't know/ unanswered
What sort of problem you've got, the probation officer will help sort it out	62	24	5	5	4	1
When you're on probation, if you ever think of getting into trouble, the probation officer is always there to talk to	66	17	7	5	3	3
My probation officer helps me to come to terms with things that happened to me in the past	53	20	12	7	6	3
Being on probation helps to keep me out of trouble with the law	45	22	12	8	13	1
Being on probation will help me to stop offending altogether	37	20	13	12	16	2

Table 4.8 *Views about respondents' probation officers*

Row percentages
(n=1,213)

	Agree strongly	Agree slightly	Neither agree nor disagree	Disagree slightly	Disagree strongly	Don't know/ unanswered
PO is always patient with me	81	12	2	3	1	1
PO tries to push me into doing things I don't want to do	4	6	4	14	73	1
I can trust PO not to tell other people things I have told in confidence	75	10	5	2	4	4
PO stands up for me when needed	51	18	18	2	3	8
PO doesn't really care about what happens to me	3	5	5	12	73	3
PO talks down to me	3	5	3	9	78	2
PO is completely straight-talking with me	80	13	2	2	1	1
PO always seems to be in a rush	4	8	4	15	68	1
I think of PO as a friend	50	28	11	5	5	2
PO really listens to me	77	15	2	2	2	1

There were, on the whole, high levels of agreement with the positive statements about probation officers and high levels of disagreement with the negative statements. Probation officers are seen in a good light; they are patient, trustworthy, caring and supportive (on the other hand, they were not perceived as pushing offenders to do things they did not want to – which may suggest that probation officers are not challenging enough). Once again, women and respondents aged 36 or over were more likely to express high levels of agreement. Although the numbers were too small for statistical tests (n=46), black offenders were consistently less likely than whites or Asians to see their probation officers positively.

A follow-up question asked about any other things which respondents might say to describe their probation officer and here fulsome praise was the order of the day. While it must be remembered that probationers with negative views may have been less likely to participate in the survey only about five per cent of respondents found anything negative to say about their supervising officer. Instead, such terms as 'friendly', 'pleasant', 'helpful', 'tolerant', 'compassionate', 'considerate', 'honest' and even 'brilliant and 'wonderful' were used. Part of the reason for such praise must be related to the fact that respondents felt that their officers were available to them at almost any time of the day if they needed to contact them: more than 60 per cent felt that they could contact their probation officer at any time at all or most times. Those who answered "most times" or "only in an emergency" were asked if they would like their PO to be available to talk to them more often, but only 17 per cent said yes.

Indeed, levels of communication between probation officers and offenders seemed to be impressively high: about three-quarters of the sample felt that they could always talk to their probation officer if they were worried about something, and that they could be completely honest and frank with him/her. Similar proportions claimed that there was real understanding between the PO and the offender, and that there was nothing they would be unwilling or embarrassed to talk about. On the whole, younger offenders were rather less confident than older ones about communicating with their PO (see Tables A.14 to A.18 in the Appendix). One further possible measure of satisfaction with probation officers may be that very few respondents had asked for a change of officer.

Perhaps as a result of this considerable level of clear and comprehensible communication, 72 per cent of respondents said that being on probation had helped them understand their offending behaviour; only nine per cent said they still did not understand this, while 15 per cent said that they had already understood their behaviour before their current order (older offenders were more likely than younger ones to say this). Indeed, almost two-thirds (63%) of the sample said that they thought being on probation would help them stay out of trouble in the future; 16 per cent said that it would not, while 13 per cent said that it would depend. These responses are similar to those given to the slightly different questions shown in Table 4.7.

On the whole, then, probation is seen as helpful and beneficial – especially in terms of providing someone to talk to (and it should be borne in mind that the characteristics of respondents suggested that they presented many problems). It was difficult to find negative comments about probation or probation officers, and there seems to have been high levels of communication between offenders and probation officers. This contrasts with findings from the National Prison Survey (Dodd and Hunter, 1992) where around two-fifths of prisoners thought that prison officers treated them well, but a similar proportion agreed with the statement that prison officers did not really care about prisoners.

5 Community service, added requirements, compliance and breach

In this chapter, the views of respondents on community service and conditions added to probation orders are discussed, as are views about the likelihood of completing the order, offending and breach.

Added conditions

Over the years it has become possible to add various conditions to probation orders. In recent times the usual purpose has been to make the basic order more rigorous for more serious offenders. Respondents were asked about their experiences of such added requirements.

In 1993, around 28 per cent of probation orders had an additional requirement, the most common of which was to participate in specified activities. In our sample, 40 per cent of respondents claimed to have additional requirements, with specified activities the most common. It was noted earlier that there seemed to be some confusion about whether such programmes were an added condition of their order or they were being attended voluntarily, and this should be borne in mind in what follows.

Only 52 respondents (4%) said that they had had to live at a probation hostel as a condition of their order, and 14 of those were still living there at the time of the interview. Most of those with a hostel condition had lived there (or expected to live there) for more than two months (68%), while for a further 29 per cent it had been for between one and two months.

Although the number of respondents with a hostel condition was small, it is worth noting the most commonly mentioned good points and bad points about hostels. Good points included having people around you, a roof over your head, being with others in a similar situation, and having things to do (snooker, television); bad points mentioned included the rules, not being allowed out late, having to mix with bad people, and lack of privacy.

Rather more respondents (27%) had attended a group of some kind as a condition of their order, with men more likely than women to have done so (31% compared with 11%). Of those with experience of group work, 30 per cent were attending a group at the time of the interview. As noted in the previous chapter, groups which dealt with alcohol problems were the most commonly attended (33%), while groups looking at offending behaviour (21%) and motor projects (23%) were also used often. Those who had attended a group were asked what they considered to be the good points about it: 20 per cent mentioned that it had raised their awareness and made them think; 17 per cent mentioned specifically that it had increased their awareness of the effects of alcohol consumption; 15 per cent said that it was useful to find out how others felt and that you could relate to this; 12 per cent said that it had helped with specific problems (apart from alcohol). Others mentioned liking the activities offered, the staff, or simply that it was something to do. Women particularly seemed to appreciate the social aspect of groups. The bad points about groups were also explored, although 39 per cent stated that there were no bad points. The most commonly mentioned bad points were the inconvenience of attending (14%), boredom (10%), that the group was not relevant to the respondent (9%), that it did not function well (7%). Only two per cent of respondents mentioned that they had not felt confident enough to participate in the group and a similar percentage said that the sessions were too intense and had made the respondent anxious.

Only seven per cent of the sample had attended a probation centre as a condition of their order, with those aged 16 to 20 more likely than older age groups to have done so, and women slightly less likely than men. For those with a probation centre requirement, most had attended for three days per week (34%), although 32 per cent claimed to have attended for only one day per week; sixteen per cent attended for two days per week, nine per cent for four days and five per cent for five days.

The experience of probation centres was very positive, but the most commonly mentioned good points about the centres focused on the social nature of attending (33% mentioned that it was something to do, 18% that they enjoyed the activities, 16% that it was useful to find out how other people felt); comments relevant to offending behaviour were much less common (5% said that the centre had made them more aware about their offending, 6% mentioned help with alcohol problems). As might have been expected, the bad points about centres followed the same pattern as the bad points about attending groups: 39 per cent said there were no bad points, and others mentioned inconvenience, boredom, lack of relevance, and sessions which were too intense.

Finally, 50 respondents (4%) said that they had been (or currently were) involved in other activities as a condition of their order. Most of these involved attendance at a psychiatric clinic/psychotherapy (13 respondents), or attendance at a drugs clinic (9 respondents).

Bad points about such additional requirements included the inconvenience of having to attend, boredom and lack of relevance to the respondent. Negative aspects, however, were greatly outnumbered by perceived good points. For specified activities, the good points seemed to be more focused on offenders' problems, while in the case of probation centres the good points seemed to revolve around the more social aspects of attending centres.

Community service

Twelve per cent of the sample had received a combination order and a section of the questionnaire asked about the experiences of this group on the community service part of the order.

In their last session of community service, 82 per cent had been working in a group, 10 per cent had been working alone, and five per cent had been working in a session run by an agency other than probation. Older respondents were more likely than younger ones, to have been working alone. Table 5.1 shows the kinds of work which respondents said they were involved in.

Painting and decorating was the most common form of work (this was also the case in the study of community service carried out by McIvor, 1992), followed by gardening. Women were less likely than men to have been involved in either of these two activities, and the oldest age group was much less likely to be involved in painting and decorating than the 16 to 20 group. On the other hand, those aged 36 or more were more likely to have worked with the elderly and made toys or crafts than were young offenders. It should be noted that the differences mentioned in this paragraph do not reach statistical significance because the sample is small.

On the whole, these activities seem very typical of community service work and may appear unimaginative, though the difficulties of finding work should not be forgotten.

Table 5.1 Work carried out on community service, by age and sex of respondent

(multiple responses possible)

	Male	Female	16–20	21–35	36 or more	All
	%	%	%	%	%	%
Painting and decorating	42	27	56	37	27	40
Gardening	31	21	28	30	30	29
Outdoor maintenance work	12	3	11	10	14	11
Helping the elderly	12	10	5	12	17	11
Helping disabled people	3	8	0	6	0	4
Working with children	2	5	0	2	9	2
Making toys/ crafts	11	14	11	11	17	12
Other activities	16	17	13	16	19	16
n	139	23	40	98	24	162

Those who had done some community service as part of their order were asked what were the good points of this. One-quarter said that there were no good points at all, but others mentioned the opportunity to do some kind of constructive work (22%), the opportunity to learn new skills and gain experience (18%), the opportunity to meet others (18%), the fact that it was something to do or somewhere to go (16%), or simply talked generally about the enjoyableness of community service. As for the bad points about community service, 19 per cent thought there were none, although 35 per cent saw it as an inconvenience and restriction of liberty, 11 per cent mentioned having to work for no pay, and nine per cent said it was boring and a waste of time.

Respondents were asked if they thought there were ways in which community service could be improved; 50 per cent said yes. This group was then asked how community service might be improved and five answers emerged: by providing a wider range of work; by being given more choice about what was to be done while on CS; by providing more equipment and resources; by being given some payment for the work; and by being given more help in finding a permanent job.

Overall, then, community service seemed to be seen in a fairly positive light, though not quite so positively as the various conditions which might be added to orders. Respondents spoke of constructive work and learning new skills, although half thought that community service could be improved. Inconvenience was the most commonly mentioned bad point about CS, although this is certainly part of the punishment. These results are similar to those of McIvor (1992) who carried out a detailed study of community service in Scotland; her respondents too were very positive about the experience of community service.

Getting through the order

Like any community penalty, being on probation does not, of course, incapacitate offenders from further offending in the way that imprisonment does. When asked whether they had committed any offences since beginning their current probation order 32 per cent of the sample said that they had. Table 5.2 shows how responses were distributed according to age and sex.

Young offenders were considerably more likely than older ones to have carried out further offences (the peak age for offending is in the late teen years), while women were less likely than men to have done so. The unemployed, and those whose current offence was burglary or theft were more likely to have committed further offences. Only 15 per cent of those who had never taken drugs had offended while on probation.

Most of those who had committed further offences claimed that their PO knew about such offending: 70 per cent said that their PO knew about all such offences, while nine per cent said that he/she knew about some of them. Only 21 per cent (81 respondents) said that their PO did not know about their offending; one-quarter of those aged 16 to 20 fell into this category, but only six per cent of those aged 36 or over. So while a not insignificant minority admitted to further offending, most of these said that their probation officer was aware of this – which must be seen as a step in the right direction. From the questions asked in the survey it is not possible to say what action, if any, probation officers were taking, nor whether the further offences known to probation officers were also known by the police.

Table 5.2 Whether or not further offences had been committed, by age and sex of respondent

	Male	Female	16–20	21–24	25–29	30–39	40 or older	All
	%	%	%	%	%	%	%	%
Further offences committed since beginning current order	34	25	46	41	33	25	11	32
No offences committed since beginning current order	65	75	53	58	66	74	89	67
Can't say/ unanswered	1	1	1	1	1	1	0	1
n	996	214	255	278	235	267	177	1,213

Further offending might be one way of predicting whether or not a probation or combination order would not be completed satisfactorily; another might be whether the offender considered the order to be fair or not. It is notable that three-quarters of the sample felt that the length of their current order was fair, while 21 per cent felt that it was not. Black and Asian offenders were more likely than white offenders to see the length of their orders as unfair, as were those who were in the early stages of their order, or those on probation for the first time. Those who considered the length of their order to be unfair were asked to provide reasons for this. By far the most common reason given was that the order was longer than the seriousness of the offence merited (66%). Other reasons mentioned were that probation was not helping in any way; that time had already been served while the offender was remanded in custody; that the terms of the order had been fulfilled and that it should be terminated. Remarkably, a few respondents said that their order should have been longer given the seriousness of the offence.

Nine out of ten respondents thought that it was very likely that they would complete their order, and six per cent thought it fairly likely. Those who had had unsettled childhoods (that is those who were fostered or in care, or in custody under 21) were slightly less likely to feel that they would complete their order. Confidence about completing the order was not related to the length of order, but it was related to whether respondents felt that the length of the order was fair or not. For those who considered the length of their order was fair, 91 per cent said that they were likely to complete; while for those who thought it unfair, 87 per cent said they were likely to complete – a small, but statistically significant difference.

Table 5.3 shows the reasons given by those who felt it likely that they would complete their order.

One in five offered the pragmatic reason that they were close to the end of their order; and almost as many implied a deterrent effect insofar as they were worried about going back to court and being sent to prison. Several responses suggested that the supervision process had been experienced as positive: probation was helpful; the respondent had enjoyed visiting his/her probation officer; completing the order would be a personal achievement.

To sum up, while one-third said they had offended during their current order (and this was most likely if the respondent was in the 16 to 20 age group), most of these said their probation officer was aware of this reoffending. Most considered their order to be fair and, partly as a result of this and a combination of pragmatic and appreciative reasons nine out of ten thought that it was very likely that they would complete their order satisfactorily.

Breaches of current orders

The way in which community penalties are enforced by probation officers is a key factor in how they are perceived, and therefore used, by the courts. A strict breach policy which is firmly adhered to is likely to increase sentencers' confidence in the relevant penalties. Probation officers have had considerable discretion in the past about how to deal with breaches and one reason for the introduction of National Standards was to make breach practice more consistent. The 1992 version of the Standards (in force during this study) stated that 'breach action should normally be taken after no more than three instances of failure to comply with the order'. It should be noted that since the implementation of the Criminal Justice Act 1991 further offending no longer leads to an automatic breach of a current community sentence. Failure to comply consists largely of non-attendance without permission. The questionnaire asked a series of questions about breaches and the reactions of probation officers to these.

Table 5.3 Reasons given for thinking it likely that the order would be completed - percentages mentioning different reasons
(multiple responses possible)

	Male	Female	16-20	21-35	36 or more	All
Order nearly completed	20	22	20	22	17	20
Frightened of going to prison/ going back to court/ other consequences	18	19	19	20	12	18
Probation is helpful/ doing good	15	21	15	15	18	16
Will not reoffend	16	9	13	14	18	14
Court requires it/ no choice	12	11	9	12	14	12
Regards completing as a personal achievement	9	8	9	8	10	9
Enjoys visiting PO/ being on probation	7	11	9	7	8	8
Wants to get probation over/ return to normal	7	5	10	6	4	6
Self or circumstances have changed	6	3	2	7	5	5
Does not find probation difficult	5	2	6	4	5	5
Does not want to let others down (PO or family)	2	1	2	2	4	2
Has completed successfully before	2	0	1	2	3	2
n	996	214	255	697	260	1,213

More than half of the sample admitted that since starting their current order they had failed to turn up for a supervision session without permission from their probation officer; males were more likely than females to have done this (56% compared with 47%), and young offenders more likely than older ones (62% of those aged 16 to 20 compared with 38% of those aged 36 or more). Those who had at some time taken drugs were more likely to have missed sessions (62% compared with 39%). The unemployed and those with no technical qualifications were also less likely to turn up at sessions.

The 162 respondents who had been sentenced to a combination order were asked whether they had ever failed to turn up for a community service session without permission: almost half (48%) admitted that they had. There was a considerable difference between those aged 36 or over and the 16 to 20 age group; for the former group 33 per cent admitted to having missed a session, but for the latter the figure was 68 per cent.

A small number of respondents (98) were currently attending a group of some kind as part of their probation order and half of these had failed to turn up for a session without permission; again, those aged 36 or over were least likely to have missed a session.

Respondents were asked whether, since commencing their order, they had been warned that their probation officers were considering taking them back to court for breaching the order. Almost one-fifth of the whole sample (19%) had been warned. The proportion of those on a combination order who had been warned was higher at 30 per cent. As might be expected given the patterns of attendance noted above, there was also a considerable difference between those aged 36 or over, where only seven per cent had been so warned, and those aged 16 to 20, where almost one-quarter (24%) had been warned. Of those who had never taken drugs only 12 per cent had been warned, compared with 23 per cent of those who had taken drugs at some time. Single people, the unemployed, those convicted of burglary and those still offending were all more likely to have been warned, as were those with an added day centre condition.

For most of those who had been warned about breach, the reason was for repeated failure to attend probation supervision sessions (75%); nine per cent had been warned for failure to attend community service sessions, and three per cent for failure to attend group sessions. (It should be remembered that those on community service only were not included in the survey.)

Only 67 respondents (6%) had actually been breached. The likelihood of being breached decreased with age, only one per cent of those aged over 35 having been breached. As for warnings, breach was more likely for those on a combination order (12%), single people, the unemployed, those still offending, those convicted of burglary and those required to attend a day centre. More than three-quarters of the reasons given for breach were failures to attend.

Generally, it looks as if there were quite a number of failures to attend sessions amongst the respondents. Young offenders were most likely to fail to turn up, while those aged 36 or more were most reliable. One-fifth of the sample had been warned of the possibility of breach action, but this had taken place for only six per cent – more than one-third of whom were in the 16 to 20 age group.

Attitudes towards offending

A majority of the sample (82%) had previous convictions. These offenders were asked why they started to offend. The most common reason given was that it was a result of peer pressure (32%); this was more likely to be mentioned by young offenders (42%) than those aged 36 or over (25%). Other popular reasons were that it was because money/'things' were needed (25%, with women more likely than men to mention this), a result of boredom or unemployment (17%), due to problems at home (14%), or as a result of stupidity or lack of thought (10%). A similar range of factors were mentioned by prisoners in the National Prison Survey, although having no money was the most commonly mentioned for this group (Dodd and Hunter, 1992).

All respondents were asked about the reasons for committing their current offence and Table 5.4 shows those most often mentioned, broken down by the age and sex of the respondent.

Interestingly, peer pressure – which was the most commonly cited reason for committing the first offence – was much less likely to be claimed as a reason for committing the current offence (7%). Needing money/'things' was mentioned by 28 per cent of respondents, with women and young offenders more likely to mention this than men or older age groups. The second most popular reason – the influence of alcohol (19%) – was rarely mentioned by female respondents, but was a common response by those aged over 35. Women and older respondents were more likely to cite mental or emotional problems as a reason for their offence.

Table 5.4 Reasons for committing the current offence, by age and sex of respondent - percentages mentioning particular reasons
(multiple responses possible)

	Male	Female	16–20	21–24	25–29	30–39	40 or older	All
Needed things or money	25	41	35	29	31	24	18	28
Under influence of alcohol	22	9	16	18	17	20	28	19
Needed drugs or under influence of drugs	13	13	10	18	16	11	6	13
Family problems	12	11	7	12	9	18	14	12
Provoked/ self-defence/ revenge/ led on by victim	9	10	12	8	9	8	9	9
Depression/mental or emotional problems	8	13	2	5	7	16	16	9
Stupidity/recklessness/ messing about/got carried away/ things got out of hand	8	3	7	10	7	5	8	7
Led on by others/ peer pressure	6	10	14	10	5	2	2	7
Temptation/ thought wouldn't get caught	7	2	9	5	4	7	5	6
Respondent claims to be wrongfull convicted	6	5	5	6	3	6	9	6
Bored/ unemployed/ nothing to do	6	3	8	4	5	5	3	5
To help family or friend/ coerced or blackmailed	4	8	3	3	5	7	4	5
n	993	213	255	276	235	266	176	1,208

More than two-fifths of the sample said that if, in future, they thought they were going to be put on probation that would stop them committing an offence (44%); just over one-third said that it would not (38%). The reasons behind these responses were probed and in the case of those who said they *would* stop, 19 per cent said it was because they did not want to be in trouble again and 13 per cent claimed that it was due to probation being inconvenient and a restriction on liberty. For those who said they *would not* stop, 18 per cent said it was because they did not regard probation as a deterrent, seven per cent said it was because they offended on the spur of the moment, and six per cent claimed that probation was not particularly demanding.

A similar set of questions were put to all respondents about the potential impact of community service, with 49 per cent stating that the thought of such a sentence would stop them committing an offence (33% said it would not). The three most commonly mentioned reasons for CS being likely to stop further offending were that it was inconvenient and a restriction on liberty (16%), that the respondent would not want to do unpleasant and demanding work (10%), and that he/she would not want to work for nothing (9%). When CS was not seen as an obstacle to future offending ten per cent said it was because CS was not seen as a deterrent, six per cent that it was not especially restrictive or demanding, and five per cent mentioned the fact that their offending was spur-of-the-moment.

Everyone was also asked whether the thought of being sent to prison would stop them committing an offence and 76 per cent said that it would. Fifteen per cent said that it would not, and men were almost twice as likely as women to say this (16% compared with 9%).

Where reference was made to prison as being most likely to stop further offending, the reasons given for this were essentially negative: that prison was a waste of one's life, that it would have an impact on the family and children (women were particularly concerned about this), that prison had a bad reputation, that the respondent would not be able to cope with prison. By far the most common reason given for probation helping to stop further offending was that being on probation helped you to understand why you had committed an offence.

A further question asked what sort of sentence would be most likely to help stop offending in future: 49 per cent said a prison sentence (either of an unspecified length or up to five years), 19 per cent said probation or community service, and 12 per cent said any sentence or that they would not need any further sentence. Interpretation of these figures, however, is clouded by some ambiguity in the question, which could be taken to refer to deterrence or to treatment.

In summary, there were clear differences between the reasons given for starting to offend and those offered for committing the current offence, with peer pressure being most important at the start but a need for money becoming significant later. Fewer than half the sample saw probation or community service as a deterrent to further offending, while three-quarters saw prison as a definite threat; prison's effect was viewed in negative terms, however, while probation was viewed more positively.

Family, friends and offending

Slightly more than two-fifths (42%) of respondents said that a member of their family had been convicted of a criminal offence (the comparable figure from the National Prison Survey is 43%); this was less likely to be the case for those aged 36 or over (26%). Table 5.5 shows the rates at which different family members were convicted. In the majority of cases, the family member was a brother/sister, with a parent the next most commonly mentioned. A spouse and a son/daughter were considerably more likely to be mentioned by women than by men. Unsurprisingly, for those aged 16 to 20, 22 per cent mentioned a parent, compared to only five per cent of those aged 36 or more; and for this latter group, eight per cent mentioned a son/daughter.

Table 5.5 Percentages of probationers with family members who had been convicted/imprisoned

(multiple responses possible)

	Male	Female	16–20	21–35	36 or more	All
Husband/ wife/ partner	1 (*)	14 (11)	3 (2)	4 (3)	3 (*)	3 (2)
Parent	14 (10)	14 (9)	22 (16)	15 (10)	5 (4)	4 (10)
Brother/ sister	32 (22)	24 (17)	31 (18)	36 (26)	16 (11)	30(21)
Uncle/ aunt	4 (4)	6 (5)	8 (7)	4 (4)	2 (1)	4 (4)
Cousin	4 (3)	3 (2)	4 (3)	4 (3)	2 (1)	3 (3)
Son/ daughter	1 (1)	5 (2)	0 (0)	*(0)	8 (4)	2 (1)
Other relative	4 (3)	6 (5)	5 (4)	5 (3)	2 (2)	4 (3)
No relative convicted/ imprisoned	58 (67)	58 (65)	54 (64)	54 (62)	74 (80)	58(67)
n	996	214	255	697	260	1,213

The first figure is for family members convicted, that in brackets is for those imprisoned.

About a third of respondents had a family member who had served a prison sentence, as Table 5.5 also shows. Most of those who had been imprisoned were close family, chiefly siblings followed by parents. Although the percentages are larger, National Prison Survey data show that for prisoners siblings and parents were also the most likely family members to have been imprisoned. One in ten of all female probationers had a husband or partner who had served time in prison.

It was not only family members who had been involved in criminal activity, however. Almost three-quarters of the sample said that they had friends who had been in trouble with the law. For those aged 16 to 20, the proportion rose to almost 90 per cent; for women and those aged 36 or more the proportion fell, but was still more than half of the sample (63% and 54% respectively). When asked to give a rough idea of how many people they knew like this who had been in trouble with the law, 31 per cent said between one and nine individuals; women were more likely than men (47% compared with 29%), and those aged 36 or over were more likely than young offenders (42% compared with 29%) to fall into this category. A further 17 per cent mentioned numbers between 10 and 19, and 13 per cent said between 20 and 29. Fifteen per cent said they knew 60 or more people who had been in trouble with the law (16% of males and 6% of females), and even allowing for a degree of exaggeration this suggests involvement with fairly widespread criminal cultures.

In nine out of ten cases, respondents' families were aware that the respondent was on probation. Women were slightly more likely than men to say that the family did not know (14% compared with 9%), and the older the respondent the more likely the family was not to know (19% of those aged 36 or over compared with 3% of those aged 16 to 20). Family views about the respondent being on probation were mixed: 27 per cent said that their family did not care, 26 per cent said that the family response was that probation was good for them, 15 per cent said the response was that they were lucky not to be in prison, and the same percentage reported that their family was shocked and disgusted. Women were more likely than men to report this last response.

In 85 per cent of cases respondents said that their friends knew they were on probation; once again women and those aged 36 or over were most likely to say that their friends did not know this. Friends' views about the respondent being on probation were less mixed than those of the family; 52 per cent reported that their friends did not care, while nine per cent said that their friends' response was that they were lucky not to be in prison.

Both family and friends of respondents were quite likely to have been in trouble with the law; mixing with offenders was, therefore, not uncommon. And neither family nor friends were particularly shocked by the respondent being on probation – the most likely response to this was to ignore it.

6 Conclusions

The survey of offenders on probation reported in this study is the first occasion on which a large sample of probationers has been asked for their views of probation and probation officers. As such, it cannot provide the depth of detail found in previous studies where small samples of offenders were interviewed (e.g. Day, 1981; Fielding, 1986). Instead, and as is the case for most sample surveys, this study offers a snapshot of offenders' views of probation in the early 1990s – a key time for the probation service – and this can also stand as a benchmark for future work.

In this final chapter we set out the salient findings of the survey and discuss these briefly in terms of their meaning for probation. It may be worth emphasising again that this study did not cover offenders on community service orders alone and therefore the results cannot be extrapolated to include this group (although those with combination orders were included). In addition, the probation service has been subjected to considerable change in the past ten years or so. If this continues, with, for example, changes in probation officer training, and the introduction of curfew orders with electronic monitoring, the results of this survey may become outdated quickly. These warnings are not meant in any way to diminish the results of the survey; as the first national exercise of this kind the results are important in themselves.

There is no doubt that probation supervision and probation officers are seen in a very positive light by offenders. Previous studies have found this to be the case - albeit for different reasons - and this survey provides confirmation of earlier findings. Such a finding may not please those who desire probation to be more punitive. However, offenders who see probation in a positive light are more likely to turn up for meetings with their probation officers, more willing to listen, and more likely to try to put into practice what is suggested to them. If probation were to be seen negatively offenders would be more likely to fail to appear for supervision. This would lead to increased breach action and - ultimately - increases in the custodial population.

There is little doubt that probation can become more rigorous and demanding without losing its basic character (see Mair et al., 1994 for the example of intensive probation). May (1995) has shown that sentencers also see probation positively. The appreciation of probation by offenders should not be ignored or forgotten. Nor should it be ignored that not all of those interviewed were equally positive about probation; older respondents and female respondents were generally more positive than young male offenders (and, although numbers were small, black respondents were most negative of all about probation). This suggests that probation officers may have to use a different approach for such offenders. Similarly, the fact that 27 per cent of the effective sample failed to keep appointments for the survey interview should not be forgotten. It is likely that this group represents those who were *not* favourable towards probation and if they had been interviewed there may have been more negative comments. It cannot simply be assumed that this percentage of offenders fails to keep appointments with their probation officers regularly (though half the sample admitted to having missed sessions), but if anything approaching this proportion is failing to turn up then this not only raises serious questions about breach, but about how probation officers can possibly organise their work effectively. Further research might be usefully carried out into this issue.

Previous research has demonstrated the deprived background of those on probation (see Stewart and Stewart, 1993) and the survey provides confirmation of this. Most respondents were not working and dependent on state benefits; they had difficulty paying bills, were poorly qualified educationally and not particularly healthy. A significant minority had spent time in care as a child. There is little doubt amongst criminologists that such factors are associated with offending although the precise relationship between them remains unclear. Their presence cannot, therefore, be ignored by probation officers and much probation work is focused on trying to alleviate the problems caused by such characteristics. In terms of their background, probationers are very similar to prisoners.

For the most part National Standards seemed to be followed, but the responses of offenders suggest that in a minority of cases the 1992 Standards were not being met. How much more difficult will it be to keep to the stricter 1995 Standards? And if Standards are not being met, what are the reasons for this? The study by Ellis et al. (1996) on enforcement suggests that probation officers sometimes employ the Standards loosely. As most monitoring systems rely on records made by officers, departures from Standards could be difficult to detect.

What happened on probation? Offending behaviour was the most commonly discussed topic during supervision, although other matters related to the characteristics of offenders were also talked about – employment, accommodation, money, personal and family problems.

Groupwork was not uncommon, and outside agencies were used frequently. Such a picture of probation work will not be surprising to those who are familiar with the service. The key question becomes how such subjects are covered; after all, most respondents seemed to be unsure about whether probation would stop them from further offending. Thus, how different topics are introduced, how their relevance to the offender is stressed, and how offenders understand these matters, become crucial questions for research into the effectiveness of probation.

While offending behaviour is discussed often during supervision, it is odd that no-one considered that their current sentence had been made in order to stop further offending. Perhaps the courts could emphasise this in passing sentence, and probation officers could make sure that this is mentioned repeatedly as a major aim of supervision. Most offenders considered that they understood their offending behaviour better as a result of probation supervision, yet one-third had committed further offences since being on probation. Respondents felt that prison was much more likely to stop further offending than probation or community service – a perception which is at odds with the evidence of reconviction rates (see Lloyd, Mair and Hough 1994). How such paradoxes might be resolved – indeed, whether they can be resolved satisfactorily – is unclear, but the need for further research is obvious.

While many of the issues which have emerged from the findings of the survey have implications for work with offenders, three in particular may be worth noting. First, reasons given for offending change over time; second, the family and friends of offenders seem to be fairly heavily involved in criminal activity; and third, drugs and alcohol play a significant role in the lives of respondents. These issues need to be taken into account by probation officers in their work with offenders both at the assessment stage and as part of supervision.

Overall, the message contained in this report is a good one for the probation service; it is viewed favourably by most of those it supervises, and seems to work hard at trying to achieve its formal aims and objectives as stated in the National Standards. However, this should not lead to any sense of complacency. It is arguable that any agency which provided similar help to that provided by the probation service to the poor and unemployed would be seen in an equally positive light. The high rate of failed survey appointments almost certainly means that those most critical of probation were not included in the survey; and young male offenders, who commit most offences and reoffend most frequently, were not as satisfied with probation as other respondents. The service is also facing budgetary restrictions which may, ultimately, have an impact upon the supervision of offenders. But despite such caveats, this survey (along with the results of court satisfaction surveys) provides a good foundation for the service to build upon and improve its services to offenders. The previous 12 years have been a period of unprecedented change for the probation service but, according to offenders, it remains in good shape to confront the future with confidence.

Appendix A: Additional tables

Table A.1 Marital status, by age of respondent, compared with prisoners and the general population

| | 16–20 | | | 21–24 | | | 25–29 | | | 30–39 | | | 40–49 | | | 50–59 | | | 60 or over | | | All | |
	Prob	Pris	Pop	Prob	Pris	Pop	Prob	Pris	Pop	Prob	Pris	Pop	Prob	Pris	Pop	Prob	Pris	Pop	Prob	Pris	Pop	Prob	Pris
Single	79	81	97	70	63	66	55	46	29	33	34	12	16	24	6	11	22	5	5	21	7	52	50
Married/as married	19	17	3	27	31	32	37	42	66	38	43	81	44	39	85	46	41	81	48	38	59	33	35
Separated, divorced, widowed	2	1	*	3	6	2	9	12	5	29	23	7	41	36	9	43	37	13	48	42	34	16	15
n	238	705		258	827		225	825		256	858		119	427		35	144		14	48		1,145	3,844

Table A.2 Who the offender lives with/who the prisoner lived with before the imprisonment, by the age of respondent

	16-20		21-24		25-29		30-39		40-49		50-59		60 or over		All	
	Prob	Pris	Prob	Pris	Prob	Pris	Prob	Pris	Prob	Pris	Prob	Pris	Prob	Pris	Prob	Pris
	%	%	%	%	%	%	%	%	%	%	%	%	%	%	%	%
Alone	12	12	20	17	25	15	26	19	33	27	41	30	41	39	23	18
Spouse/ Partner	20	24	30	43	42	58	41	63	46	54	43	55	50	44	35	49
Parents	47	46	27	26	15	14	9	7	6	5	5	3	*	6	21	19
Other adult relations	3	4	2	5	3	4	2	3	1	4	*	3	*	*	2	4
Friends	7	9	7	7	5	6	6	5	4	4	4	4	5	6	6	6
Alone with children	2	*	7	*	10	1	7	2	5	4	4	3	4	2	6	1
Adult children only	*	*	*	*	*	*	1	*	2	1	*	1	*	2	1	*
Other	8	4	6	2	1	2	8	1	3	1	4	1	*	2	6	2
n	255	705	278	827	235	825	267	858	125	427	38	144	14	48	1,213	3,844

Table A.3 Who the offender lives with/who the prisoner lived with before imprisonment, by sex of respondent

	Males		Females		All	
	Prob	Pris	Prob	Pris	Prob	Pris
	%	%	%	%	%	%
Alone	25	18	14	14	23	18
Spouse/partner	36	49	34	43	35	49
Parents	24	20	8	11	21	19
Other adult Relations	2	4	1	6	2	4
Friends	7	6	2	7	6	6
Alone with children	1	1	32	14	6	1
Adult children only	1	*	1	2	1	*
Other	5	2	8	3	6	2
n	996	3,718	214	827	1,213	3,844

Table A.4 Highest qualification achieved, by sex of respondent

	Male	Female	All
	%	%	%
University	1	3	1
A level	3	3	3
O level	8	12	8
GCSE	11	9	10
CSE	10	13	10
Other	2	1	2
no qualifications	66	61	65
n	981	218	1,199

The categories include Scottish and other equivalent qualifications. The table shows the *highest* qualifications achieved. In the text it is assumed that those with a degree also gained A and O levels, and those with A levels also gained O levels.

Table A.5 Percentages of respondents with a driving licence, by sex of respondent, compared with general population

	Males		Females		All	
	Prob	Gen pop	Prob	Gen pop	Prob	Gen pop
17–20	12	54	20	42	13	48
21–29	23	83	23	68	23	75
30–39	29	91	38	73	31	82
40–49	37	88	31	70	37	79
All ages 17 and over	24	81	27	54	25	67
n	984		211		1,198	

Table A.6 Percentage of offenders who had been offered drugs in the past 12 months, by age and sex of respondent

	Male	Female	16–20	21–35	36 or more	All
Cannabis	52	34	65	53	23	49
Amphetamines	39	28	53	40	14	37
Temazepam	24	16	29	24	10	22
LSD	29	15	46	27	9	27
Ecstasy	27	15	38	26	8	25
Magic mushrooms	18	10	27	18	4	17
Heroin	16	13	10	19	10	15
Cocaine	17	7	14	18	9	15
Methadone	12	10	8	14	8	11
Crack	12	8	12	12	9	11
None of these drugs offered	32	50	19	29	66	35
Unanswered/blank	18	19	12	22	14	18
n	996	214	255	697	260	1,213

Table A.7 Percentages of males who indicated that they had taken particular drugs in the last year, ages 16 to 59 only, compared with results from BCS 1994.

	16–19		20–24		25–29		30–34		35–39		40–44		45–59		All 16–59	
	Prob	BCS	Prob	BCS	Prob	BCS	Prob	BCS	Prob	BCS	Prob	BCS	Prob	BCS	Prob	BCS
Cannabis	60	32	62	29	47	17	38	9	41	5	9	4	12	1	46	10
Ampheta-mines	33	12	36	12	27	4	18	2	16	*	3	*	10	*	25	3
LSD	31	7	23	7	13	2	11	1	5	*	2	*	0	0	16	2
Magic mush-rooms	23	6	15	5	10	2	8	*	6	*	2	*	0	*	11	1
Ecstasy	25	5	22	4	10	2	9	*	3	*	0	0	0	*	13	1
Temaz-pan	22	1	19	2	19	*	17	*	12	1	5	*	5	*	17	1
Cocaine	13	1	9	2	12	1	8	*	8	*	2	0	4	0	9	*
Crack	2	0	6	0	8	0	6	0	1	0	0	0	4	0	5	0
Metha-done	3	*	10	*	12	0	6	0	7	0	3	*	6	0	8	*
Heroin	5	0	10	1	14	*	11	0	6	0	3	0	4	0	9	*
n	139	48	298	380	196	576	128	662	83	621	67	517	72	1,442	983	4,446

Table A.8 Offence at first conviction, by age and sex of respondent

	Male	Female	16–20	21–24	25–29	30–39	40 or older	All
	%	%	%	%	%	%	%	%
Violence	10	11	17	15	9	6	5	11
Sexual	2	1	1	0	2	1	5	1
Burglary	27	14	32	29	24	23	17	25
Robbery	3	2	2	6	3	3	3	3
Car theft/theft from car	13	4	19	12	14	11	3	12
Other theft/ handling	20	49	24	26	22	22	25	24
Fraud, forgery, deception	4	13	3	6	7	3	9	5
Criminal damage	11	7	14	12	10	12	4	11
Drink–driving	7	1	2	5	7	7	11	6
Other driving	12	3	13	8	8	11	16	11
Drugs–related	2	3	3	2	2	1	3	2
Other	10	9	6	9	14	11	9	10
n	853	135	185	238	205	221	140	989

Table A.9 Percentage committing particular offences prior to first conviction, by age and sex of respondent

Includes only those admitting to offending before their first conviction
Multiple response possible

	Male	Female	16–20	21–24	25–29	30–39	40 or older	All
	%	%	%	%	%	%	%	%
Violence	13	10	15	11	16	12	9	13
Sexual	2	3	2	0	3	2	8	2
Burglary	37	13	38	39	28	27	35	34
Robbery	4	0	3	1	7	5	3	3
Car theft/theft from car	27	8	39	25	27	12	10	25
Other theft/ handling	39	67	44	44	44	43	25	42
Fraud, forgery, deception	4	8	6	4	5	2	10	5
Criminal damage	20	5	24	17	19	15	14	18
Drink-driving	5	3	2	1	6	8	11	4
Other driving	12	7	11	9	12	14	8	11
Drugs-related	7	10	8	10	7	6	6	8
Other	7	5	5	7	6	10	5	7
n	490	65	138	150	107	116	46	557

Table A.10 Topics discussed in last session with the probation officer, by age and sex of respondent – percentages mentioning particular topics

	Male	Female	16-20	21-24	25-29	30-39	40 or more	All
Things to do in spare time to keep out of trouble	32	23	38	37	25	20	24	29
Problems about where I live	32	31	34	36	33	28	25	31
Problems with money/debts	28	43	32	37	29	29	22	30
Employment	46	23	57	50	40	29	31	42
Problems with family	28	39	34	27	27	35	26	30
Personal problems	39	46	40	41	39	40	41	40
Why I committed the offence	22	14	29	21	16	16	20	20
How my offence affected other people	12	6	11	13	9	8	13	11
Taking drugs	16	12	12	23	18	16	5	16
Consumption of alcohol	24	9	14	22	19	23	30	21
Problems with my health	18	25	10	15	20	23	30	19
n	996	214	255	278	235	267	177	1,213

Table A.11 Help sought from agencies (other than specified programmes) – percentages seeking help

	Male	Female	16–20	21–24	25–29	30–39	40 or more	All
Health problems	12	13	4	4	15	17	25	12
Job training and work	22	15	26	22	19	16	22	21
Social and housing benefits	24	21	27	22	21	20	27	23
Social services	15	21	17	15	14	18	17	16
Reading, writing and numbers	3	1	3	3	3	3	1	3
Fitness and exercise	7	5	7	7	6	6	5	6
Addiction to drugs	9	8	3	13	10	9	5	8
Addiction to alcohol	8	2	2	5	8	10	12	7
Legal aid or advice	14	15	15	16	18	12	11	15
n	996	214	255	278	235	267	177	1,213

Table A.12 Perceived reasons for being given probation rather than another sentence

Multiple responses possible

	Male	Female	16-20	21-24	25-29	30-39	40 or more	All
	%	%	%	%	%	%	%	%
Probation would benefit respondent	26	29	31	23	28	25	26	27
Good solicitor or PSR, sympathetic sentencer	15	16	10	17	15	15	20	15
Chance to prove him/herself, second chance	13	10	17	15	13	8	7	12
Physical or emotional health	10	12	4	8	10	15	17	10
Minor offence only	11	6	7	12	8	10	11	10
First offence, or first offence for a long time	9	11	9	12	6	10	8	9
Less effect on family	6	18	6	5	9	11	8	8
In work or education	5	4	3	4	8	5	4	5
Prison failed before to stop offending	5	1	1	6	5	5	4	4
Offender asked for probation/ asked not to have another sentence	4	3	2	6	5	4	3	4
n	996	214	255	278	235	267	177	1,213

Table A.13 Percentage of respondents mentioning various bad points about probation

	Male	Female	16-20	21-24	25-29	30-39	40 or more	All
Time taken to attend	25	18	25	21	28	27	20	24
Time taken to travel	7	5	9	6	8	6	6	7
Boring/waste of time	4	3	5	5	4	4	3	4
No bad points mentioned	52	61	54	55	53	50	60	54
n	996	214	255	278	235	267	177	1,213

Table A.14 Responses to "Do you feel you can talk to your probation officer if you are worried about something?"

	Male	Female	16-20	21-24	25-29	30-39	40 or more	All
	%	%	%	%	%	%	%	%
Always	74	79	68	73	74	77	89	75
Sometimes	21	16	24	24	20	19	9	20
Never	3	3	6	2	4	2	1	3
Can't say/not answered	2	2	2	1	2	3	1	1
n	996	214	255	278	235	267	177	1,213

Table A.15 Responses to "Do you feel you can be completely honest and frank with your probation officer?"

	Male	Female	16-20	21-24	25-29	30-39	40 or more	All
	%	%	%	%	%	%	%	%
All of the time	73	69	64	70	74	74	84	72
Sometimes	22	27	28	27	20	23	14	23
Rarely or never	4	3	5	2	6	2	1	3
Can't say/not answered	1	1	2	2	0	1	1	1
n	996	214	255	278	235	267	177	1,213

Table A.16 Responses to "Does your probation officer ever use words you don't understand?"

	Male	Female	16-20	21-24	26-29	30-39	40 or more	All
	%	%	%	%	%	%	%	%
Yes, often	2	4	5	3	3	1	2	3
Yes, sometimes	21	23	36	29	17	15	9	22
No, never	76	72	59	67	81	83	90	75
Not answered	*	1	1	1	*	1	0	1
n	996	214	255	278	235	267	177	1,213

Table A.17 Responses to "Do you feel that your probation officer understands what you are really saying to him/her?"

	Male	Female	16–20	21–24	25–29	30–39	40 or more	All
	%	%	%	%	%	%	%	%
Yes, always	68	71	65	65	68	71	79	69
Yes, sometimes	24	21	25	26	23	24	17	23
No, rarely	4	4	3	5	6	2	2	4
No, never	1	2	2	1	3	1	0	1
Can't say/ not answered	3	2	5	3	1	2	2	3
n	996	214	255	278	235	267	177	1,213

Table A.18 Responses to "Is there anything you would be unwilling or embarrassed to talk about with your probation officer?"

	Male	Female	16–20	21–24	25–29	30–39	40 or more	All
	%	%	%	%	%	%	%	%
Yes, a lot of things	3	3	2	3	4	2	3	3
Yes, a few things	21	19	24	18	25	21	16	21
No	75	78	72	79	71	76	81	76
Not answered	1	1	2	1	0	1	0	1
n	996	214	255	278	235	267	177	1,213

References

Bailey, R. and Ward, D. (1992). *Probation Supervision: attitudes to formalised helping.* Belfast: Probation Board for Northern Ireland.

Bennett, N. et al. (1994). *Health Survey for England 1993.* London: HMSO.

Bridgwood, A. and Malbon, G. (1995). *Survey of the physical health of prisoners 1994.* London: HMSO.

Central Statistical Office (1994). *Social Trends 24.* London: HMSO.

Central Statistical Office (1996). *Social Trends 26.* London: HMSO.

Day, P. (1981). *Social Work and Social Control.* London: Tavistock.

Department of Transport (1995). *Transport Statistics 1995.* London: HMSO.

Ditton, J. and Ford, R. (1994). *The Reality of Probation: a formal ethnography of process and practice.* Aldershot: Avebury.

Dodd, T. and Hunter, P. (1992). *The national prison survey.* London: HMSO.

Dundon-Smith, D., Ghate, D., and Hales, J. (1994). *On Probation – a survey of offenders: Technical Report.* London: SCPR.

Ellis, T., Hedderman, C., and Mortimer, E. (1996). *Ensuring compliance and dealing with breach: a study of enforcement in the probation service.* Home Office Research Study 158. London: Home Office.

Fielding, N. (1986). *Probation Practice: client support under social control.* Aldershot: Gower.

Home Office (1992). *National Standards for the Supervision of Offenders in the Community.* London: Home Office.

Home Office (1994). *Probation Statistics England and Wales* 1993. London: Home Office.

Home Office (1995a). *Strengthening Punishment in the Community.* Cm 2780. London: HMSO.

Home Office (1995b). *National Standards for the Supervision of Offenders in the Community.* London: Home Office.

Lloyd, C., Mair, G. and Hough, M. (1994). *Explaining Reconviction Rates: a critical analysis.* Home Office Research Study 136. London: HMSO.

Mair, G. (1991). *'What Works - Nothing or Everything? Measuring the effectiveness of sentences'.* Home Office Research Bulletin 30, pp.3-8.

Mair, G. (1996). *'Developments in probation in England and Wales 1984-1993'. In G. McIvor (ed.) Working with Offenders.* Research Highlights in Social Work 26. London: Jessica Kingsley.

Mair, G., Lloyd, C., Nee, C. and Sibbitt, R. (1994). *Intensive Probation in England and Wales: an evaluation.* Home Office Research Study 133. London: HMSO.

Mantle, G. (1995). *'Probation: offenders have their say'.* Justice of the Peace and Local Government Law 368.

May, C. (1995) *Measuring the Satisfaction of Courts with the Probation Service.* Home Office Research Study 144. London: Home Office.

McIvor, G. (1992). *Sentenced to Serve: the operation and impact of community service by offenders.* Aldershot: Avebury.

Mott, J. and Mirrlees-Black, C. (1995). *Self-reported Drug Misuse in England and Wales: Findings from the 1992 British Crime Survey.* Research and Planning Unit Paper 89. London: Home Office.

Nee, C. and Sibbitt, R. (1993). *The Probation Response to Drug Misuse.* Research and Planning Unit Paper 78. London: Home Office.

Office of Population Censuses and Surveys (1994). *General Household Survey 1992.* London: HMSO.

Office of Population Censuses and Surveys (1995). *General Household Survey 1993.* London: HMSO.

Ramsay, M. and Percy, A. (1996). *Drug misuse declared: results of the 1994 British Crime Survey.* Home Office Research Study 151. London: Home Office.

Stewart, G. and Stewart, J. (1993). *Social Circumstances of Younger Offenders under Supervision.* London: Association of Chief Officers of Probation.

Willis, A. (1986). *Help and control in probation: an empirical assessment of probation practice. In* J.Pointing *(ed.) Alternatives to Custody.* Oxford: Basil Blackwell.

Publications

List of research publications

A list of research reports for the last three years is provided below. A **full** list of publications is available on request from the Research and Statistics Directorate Information and Publications Group.

Home Office Research Studies (HORS)

133. **Intensive Probation in England and Wales: an evaluation.** George Mair, Charles Lloyd, Claire Nee and Rae Sibbett. 1994. xiv + 143pp. (0 11 341114 6).

134. **Contacts between Police and Public: findings from the 1992 British Crime Survey.** Wesley G Skogan. 1995. ix + 93pp. (0 11 341115 4).

135. **Policing low-level disorder: Police use of Section 5 of the Public Order Act 1986.** David Brown and Tom Ellis. 1994. ix + 69pp. (0 11 341116 2).

136. **Explaining reconviction rates: A critical analysis.** Charles Lloyd, George Mair and Mike Hough. 1995. xiv + 103pp. (0 11 341117 0).

137. **Case Screening by the Crown Prosecution Service: How and why cases are terminated.** Debbie Crisp and David Moxon. 1995. viii + 66pp. (0 11 341137 5).

138. **Public Interest Case Assessment Schemes.** Debbie Crisp, Claire Whittaker and Jessica Harris. 1995. x + 58pp. (0 11 341139 1).

139. **Policing domestic violence in the 1990s.** Sharon Grace. 1995. x + 74pp. (0 11 341140 5).

140. **Young people, victimisation and the police: British Crime Survey findings on experiences and attitudes of 12 to 15 year olds.** Natalie Aye Maung. 1995. xii + 140pp. (0 11 341150 2).

141. **The Settlement of refugees in Britain.** Jenny Carey-Wood, Karen Duke, Valerie Karn and Tony Marshall. 1995. xii + 133pp. (0 11 341145 6).

142. **Vietnamese Refugees since 1982.** Karen Duke and Tony Marshall. 1995. x + 62pp. (0 11 341147 2).

143. **The Parish Special Constables Scheme.** Peter Southgate, Tom Bucke and Carole Byron. 1995. x + 59pp. (1 85893 458 3).

144. **Measuring the Satisfaction of the Courts with the Probation Service.** Chris May. 1995. x + 76pp. (1 85893 483 4).

145. **Young people and crime.** John Graham and Benjamin Bowling. 1995. xv + 142pp. (1 85893 551 2).

146. **Crime against retail and manufacturing premises: findings from the 1994 Commercial Victimisation Survey.** Catriona Mirrlees-Black and Alec Ross. 1995. xi + 110pp. (1 85893 554 7).

147. **Anxiety about crime: findings from the 1994 British Crime Survey.** Michael Hough. 1995. viii + 92pp. (1 85893 553 9).

148. **The ILPS Methadone Prescribing Project.** Rae Sibbitt. 1996. viii + 69pp. (1 85893 485 0).

149. **To scare straight or educate? The British experience of day visits to prison for young people.** Charles Lloyd. 1996. xi + 60pp. (1 85893 570 9).

150. **Predicting reoffending for Discretionary Conditional Release.** John B Copas, Peter Marshall and Roger Tarling. 1996. vii + 49pp. (1 85893 576 8).

151. **Drug misuse declared: results of the 1994 British Crime Survey.** Malcom Ramsay and Andrew Percy. 1996. xv + 131pp. (1 85893 628 4).

152. **An Evaluation of the Introduction and Operation of the Youth Court.** David O'Mahony and Kevin Haines. 1996. viii + 70pp. (1 85893 579 2).

153. **Fitting supervision to offenders: assessment and allocation decisions in the Probation Service.** Ros Burnett. 1996. xi + 99pp. (1 85893 599 7).

154 **Ethnic minorities: victimisation and racial harassment. Findings from the 1988 and 1992 British Crime Surveys.** Marian Fitzgerald and Chris Hale. 1996. xi + 97pp (1 85893 603 9).

155 **PACE ten years on: a review of research.** David Brown. 1997. xx + 281pp. (1 85893 603 9).

156. **Automatic Conditional Release: the first two years.** Mike Maguire, Brigitte Perroud and Peter Raynor. 1996. x + 114pp. (1 85893 659 4).

157. **Testing obscenity: an international comparison of laws and controls relating to obscene material.** Sharon Grace. 1996. ix + 46pp. (1 85893 672 1).

158. **Enforcing community sentences: supervisors' perspectives on ensuring compliance and dealing with breach.** Tom Ellis, Carol Hedderman and Ed Mortimer. 1996. x + 81pp. (1 85893 691 8).

160. **Implementing crime prevention schemes in a multi-agency setting: aspects of process in the Safer Cities programme.** Mike Sutton. 1996. x + 53pp. (1 85893 691 8).

161. **Reducing criminality among young people: a sample of relevant programmes in the United Kingdom.** David Utting. 1997. vi + 122pp. (1 85893 744 2).

162 **Imprisoned women and mothers.** Dianne Caddle and Debbie Crisp. 1996. xiii + 74pp. (1 85893 760 4)

163. **Curfew orders with electronic monitoring: an evaluation of the first twelve months of the trials in Greater Manchester, Norfolk and Berkshire, 1995 - 1996.** George Mair and Ed Mortimer. 1996. x + 50pp. (1 85893 765 5).

165. **Enforcing financial penalties.** Claire Whittaker and Alan Mackie. 1997. xii + 58pp. (1 85893 786 8).

166. **Assessing offenders' needs: assessment scales for the probation service.** Rosumund Aubrey and Michael Hough. x + 55pp.(1 85893 799 X).

167 **Offenders on probation.** George Mair and Chris May. 1997. xiv + 95pp. (1 85893 890 2).

168. **Managing courts effectively: The reasons for adjournments in magistrates' courts**. Claire Whittaker, Alan Mackie, Ruth Lewis and Nicola Ponikiewski. 1997. x + 37pp. (1 85893 804 X).

Nos 159 and 164 not published yet.

Research and Planning Unit Papers (RPUP)

86. **Drug Education Amongst Teenagers: a 1992 British Crime Survey Analysis**. Lizanne Dowds and Judith Redfern. 1995.

87. **Group 4 Prisoner Escort Service: a survey of customer satisfaction**. Claire Nee. 1994.

88. **Special Considerations: Issues for the Management and Organisation of the Volunteer Police**. Catriona Mirrlees-Black and Carole Byron. 1995.

89. **Self-reported drug misuse in England and Wales: findings from the 1992 British Crime Survey.** Joy Mott and Catriona Mirrlees-Black. 1995.

90. **Improving bail decisions: the bail process project, phase 1.** John Burrows, Paul Henderson and Patricia Morgan. 1995.

91. **Practitioners' views of the Criminal Justice Act: a survey of criminal justice agencies**. George Mair and Chris May. 1995.

92. **Obscene, threatening and other troublesome telephone calls to women in England and Wales: 1982-1992**. Wendy Buck, Michael Chatterton and Ken Pease. 1995.

93. **A survey of the prisoner escort and custody service provided by Group 4 and by Securicor Custodial Services**. Diane Caddle. 1995.

Research Findings

12. **Explaining Reconviction Rates: A Critical Analysis.** Charles Lloyd, George Mair and Mike Hough. 1995.

13. **Equal opportunities and the Fire Service.** Tom Bucke. 1994.

14. **Trends in Crime: Findings from the 1994 British Crime Survey.**
Pat Mayhew, Catriona Mirrlees-Black and Natalie Aye Maung. 1994.

15. **Intensive Probation in England and Wales: an evaluation.**
George Mair, Charles Lloyd, Claire Nee and Rae Sibbitt. 1995.

16. **The settlement of refugees in Britain.** Jenny Carey-Wood,
Karen Duke, Valerie Karn and Tony Marshall. 1995.

17. **Young people, victimisation and the police: British Crime Survey
findings on experiences and attitudes of 12- to 15- year-olds.**
Natalie Aye Maung.

18. **Vietnamese Refugees since 1982.** Karen Duke and Tony Marshall.
1995.

19. **Supervision of Restricted Patients in the Community.**
Suzanne Dell and Adrian Grounds. 1995.

20. **Videotaping children's evidence: an evaluation.** Graham Davies,
Clare Wilson, Rebecca Mitchell and John Milsom. 1995.

21. **The mentally disordered and the police.** Graham Robertson,
Richard Pearson and Robert Gibb. 1995.

22. **Preparing records of taped interviews.** Andrew Hooke and
Jim Knox. 1995.

23. **Obscene, threatening and other troublesome telephone calls
to women: Findings from the British Crime Survey.**
Wendy Buck, Michael Chatterton and Ken Pease. 1995.

24. **Young people and crime.** John Graham and Ben Bowling. 1995.

25. **Anxiety about crime: Findings from the 1994 British Crime
Survey.** Michael Hough. 1995.

26. **Crime against retail premises in 1993.** Catriona Mirrlees-Black
and Alec Ross. 1995.

27. **Crime against manufacturing premises in 1993.**
Catriona Mirrlees-Black and Alec Ross. 1995.

28. **Policing and the public: findings from the 1994 British Crime
Survey.** Tom Bucke. 1995.

29.   **The Child Witness Pack – An Evaluation.** Joyce Plotnikoff and Richard Woolfson. 1995.

30.   **To scare straight or educate? The British experience of day visits to prison for young people.** Charles Lloyd. 1996.

31.   **The ADT drug treatment programme at HMP Downview – a preliminary evaluation.** Elaine Player and Carol Martin. 1996.

32.   **Wolds remand prison – an evaluation.** Keith Bottomley, Adrian James, Emma Clare and Alison Liebling. 1996.

33.   **Drug misuse declared: results of the 1994 British Crime Survey.** Malcolm Ramsay and Andrew Percy. 1996.

34.   **Crack cocaine and drugs-crime careers.** Howard Parker and Tim Bottomley. 1996.

35.   **Imprisonment for fine default.** David Moxon and Claire Whittaker. 1996.

36.   **Fine impositions and enforcement following the Criminal Justice Act 1993.** Elizabeth Charman, Bryan Gibson, Terry Honess and Rod Morgan. 1996.

37.   **Victimisation in prisons.** Ian O'Donnell and Kimmett Edgar. 1996.

38   **Mothers in prison.** Dianne Caddle and Debbie Crisp. 1997.

39.   **Ethnic minorities, victimisation and racial harassment.** Marian Fitzgerald and Chris Hale. 1996.

40.   **Evaluating joint performance management between the police and the Crown Prosecution Service.** Andrew Hooke, Jim Knox and David Portas. 1996.

41.   **Public attitudes to drug-related crime.** Sharon Grace. 1996.

42.   **Domestic burglary schemes in the safer cities programme.** Paul Ekblom, Ho Law and Mike Sutton. 1996.

43.   **Pakistani women's experience of domestic violence in Great Britain.** Salma Choudry. 1996.

44.   **Witnesses with learning disabilities.** Andrew Sanders, Jane Creaton, Sophia Bird and Leanne Weber. 1997.

45.   **Does treating sex offenders reduce reoffending?** Carol Hedderman and Darren sugg. 1996.

46.   **Re-education programmes for violent men - an evaluation.** Russell Dobash, Rebecca Emerson Dobash, Kate Cavanagh and Ruth Lewis. 1996.

47.   **Sentencing without a pre-sentence report.** Nigel Charles, Claire Whittaker and Caroline Ball. 1997.

48   **Magistrates' views of the probation service.** Chris May. 1997.

49.   **PACE ten years on: a review of the research.** David Brown. 1997.

Research Bulletin

The Research Bulletin is published twice each year and contains short articles on recent research.

Occasional Papers

Measurement of caseload weightings associated with the Children Act. Richard J. Gadsden and Graham J. Worsdale. 1994. (Available from the RSD Information and Publications Group).

Managing difficult prisoners: The Lincoln and Hull special units. Professor Keith Bottomley, Professor Norman Jepson, Mr Kenneth Elliott and Dr Jeremy Coid. 1994. (Available from the RSD Information and Publications Group).

The Nacro diversion initiative for mentally disturbed offenders: an account and an evaluation. Home Office, NACRO and Mental Health Foundation. 1994. (Available from the RSD Information and Publications Group.)

Probation Motor Projects in England and Wales. J P Martin and Douglas Martin. 1994.

Community-based treatment of sex offenders: an evaluation of seven treatment programmes. R Beckett, A Beech, D Fisher and A S Fordham. 1994.

Videotaping children's evidence: an evaluation. Graham Davies, Clare Wilson, Rebecca Mitchell and John Milsom. 1995.

Managing the needs of female prisoners. Allison Morris, Chris Wilkinson, Andrea Tisi, Jane Woodrow and Ann Rockley. 1995.

Local information points for volunteers. Michael Locke, Nick Richards, Lorraine Down, Jon Griffiths and Roger Worgan. 1995.

Mental disorder in remand prisoners. Anthony Maden, Caecilia J. A. Taylor, Deborah Brooke and John Gunn. 1996.

An evaluation of prison work and training. Frances Simon and Claire Corbett. 1996.

The Impact of the National Lottery on the Horse-Race Betting Levy. Simon Field. 1996.

Reviewing risk. A review of research on the assessment and management of risk and dangerousness: implications for policy and practice in the Probation Service. Hazel Kemshall. 1996. (available from IPG).

Crack cocaine and drugs - crime careers. Howard Parker and Tim Bottomley. 1996.

The social implications of casino gambling. Iain Brown and Sue Fisher (edited by Clem Henricson and Joel Miller). 1996.

Evaluation of a Home Office initiative to help offenders into employment. Ken Roberts, Alana Barton, Julian Buchanan and Barry Goldson. 1996.

Books

Analysing Offending. Data, Models and Interpretations. Roger Tarling. 1993. viii + 203pp. (0 11 341080 8).

Requests for Publications

Home Office Research Studies from 143 onwards, *Research and Planning Unit Papers, Research Findings and Research Bulletins* are available **subject to availability** on request from:

Research and Statistics Directorate
Information and Publications Group
Room 201, Home Office
50 Queen Anne's Gate
London SW1H 9AT
Telephone: 0171 273 2084
Fascimile: 0171 222 0211
Internet: http://www.open.gov.uk/home off/rsdhome.htp

Occasional Papers can be purchased from:
Home Office
Publications Unit
50 Queen Anne's Gate
London SW1H 9AT
Telephone: 0171 273 2302

Home Office Research Studies prior to 143 can be purchased from:

HMSO Publications Centre

(Mail, fax and telephone orders only)
PO Box 276, London SW8 5DT
Telephone orders: 0171-873 9090
General enquiries: 0171-873 0011
(queuing system in operation for both numbers)
Fax orders: 0171-873 8200

*And also from **HMSO Bookshops***